# ROGUES & HEROES of Newport's GILDED AGE

# ROGUES & HEROES *of* Newport's GILDED AGE

EDWARD MORRIS

THE History PRESS

Published by The History Press
Charleston, SC 29403
www.historypress.net



Image are courtesy of the author unless otherwise noted.

*Front cover*: *The Newport Casino*. Lithograph by C. Graham from *Harper's Weekly* magazine, spring 1880 edition. *Courtesy Newport Tennis Hall of Fame.*

First published 2012

Manufactured in the United States

ISBN 978.1.60949.755.2

Library of Congress CIP data applied for.

*Notice*: The information in this book is true and complete to the best of our knowledge. It is offered without guarantee on the part of the author or The History Press. The author and The History Press disclaim all liability in connection with the use of this book.

# CONTENTS

# PREFACE

For Gilded Age gentlemen, the coachman was the outdoor butler, unless the gentlemen chose to walk on their own. Not only was the coachman in charge of the horses and stable hands, but he was also a travel advisor, road map expert and weather consultant, as well as a connoisseur of hotels, restaurants and entertainment venues.

Man's best friend was the horse for more than three thousand years, replacing the hunter-gatherer's dog of Charles Darwin's *On the Origin of Species*. Then the sails on ships were replaced by iron rails on steam engine trains, the Model T Ford on paved roads and now the airplane in the air. Today, those horses have been put out to pasture (except for horse races).

A gentleman's coachman knew his likes and dislikes and how to please him. And he had to know his oats to keep the horses fed and well bred. Today, anyone can Google such information on the computer.

Gilded Age gentlemen loved their horses and had plenty of them. A team of four or six horses was faster than two horses and could pull a larger and more ostentatious carriage for family and friends.

Oliver Hazard Perry Belmont, who married Alva Vanderbilt after her divorce from William K. Vanderbilt, had stables built inside Belcourt Castle for thirty-four of his beloved horses. After their marriage, she made him build separate stables for those horses, but he loved them just as much.

Gilded Age gentlemen—and ladies—liked to be in command of their families and their fortunes. You'll be reading about many of those gentlemen, like Oliver's father, August Belmont; James Gordon Bennett;

and William K. Vanderbilt. But you'll also read about Gilded Age ladies like Mrs. William Backhouse Astor Jr., Alva Erskin Smith Vanderbilt Belmont and Mrs. Stuyvesant (Mamie) Fish.

This volume is intended to put the crosscurrents of that world into a larger historical perspective, starting with one of the early leaders of New York's high society summer migration to Newport, namely August Belmont.

# ACKNOWLEDGEMENTS

I am very much indebted to the Newport Historical Society and Pieter Roos—then education director but now executive director of Doris Duke's Newport Restoration Foundation—for hiring me to research a guided tour script for Newport's Cliff Walk and to give tours for groups of Newport visitors for six years.

As a retired journalist, upon settling with my wife and son in Newport, I served as a step-on bus guide for Newport's cruise ship visitors using a script I had researched and written for this purpose.

It was titled "The Coachman's Guide to Newport" and is the foundation of what you are now reading. I had shown it to Pieter Roos when he engaged me to research a guided tour script of Cliff Walk (that tour book, *A Guide to Newport's Cliff Walk*, has since sold more than seven thousand copies over the past twelve years).

To spice up this previously unpublished "Coachman's Guide to Newport," I have added the stories of the rogues and heroes of the world that Samuel Langhorne Clemens, author of *Tom Sawyer* and *Huckleberry Finn*, so aptly called "gilded" because he knew so very well that "it was certainly not *solid gold*, but rather a very thin dusting of that metal that glistens in the sun!" Clemens used his business pseudonym, Mark Twain, when he wanted to be publicly recognized.

I am also deeply indebted to my son, Robert, for countless suggestions and all the numerous photographs taken by him and his very gracious friend Marsha Hanson.

*I*

# HISTORY OF COLONIAL NEWPORT

Welcome to Newport, the first vacation resort in America. Already by the 1720s, so many plantation owners from the southern colonies and the West Indies were coming to enjoy Newport's cool summer breezes that they affectionately called this town the "Carolina Hospital." They said that the late evening and early morning fogs helped to keep the mosquitoes at bay and thus prevented "the fever." And French officers stationed here during the American Revolution credited those fogs for the beautiful glowing cheeks of Newport girls. Perhaps you've noticed them already?

Newport is on the island of Aquidneck, the Indian word for island. The five- by fifteen-mile island is in Rhode Island, the smallest state (only thirty-five by sixty-five miles). And just before the American Revolution, with a population of 11,500 and a volume of trade exceeding that of New York, it was an important setting for wealthy merchants, smugglers, privateers and even pirates—thirty-one of whom were hanged by the neck on Gravel Point, near Long Wharf, in only one six-month period. In fact, its British detractors sometimes called the state "Rogue's Island."

And the volume of Newport trade, which included such things as rum, slaves, molasses, sugar, candles and handcrafted products, had expanded so much over more than one hundred years that by 1760 it exceeded the total volume of New York City's trade and began to rival that of the other major colonial ports of Boston, Philadelphia and Charleston, South Carolina.

## SIX THOUSAND BRITISH TROOPS OCCUPY NEWPORT

Newport's first Golden Age ended with the American Revolution, which brought Newport a three-year occupation by six thousand British troops followed seven months later by a one-year occupation by a similar number of troops of French-allied general Comte de Rochambeau.

During the British stay, Newport's population plummeted from 9,000 to 4,500, and to keep warm, the British soldiers tore down some 400 vacant houses (there were 1,100 houses here then) just to burn the lumber as firewood. But some 300 of those pre-revolutionary houses are still standing in Newport—maybe 40 percent of those still surviving in the thirteen original states.

Newport also has ten buildings predating 1700, including the White Horse Tavern, claimed to be the oldest in the country where you can still eat and drink. The fourth-oldest state capitol building is here, the oldest Jewish synagogue is here, the oldest private library still lending books from its original building is here and the first street to be lit by gaslight, in 1803, is here—along with much more.

After the Revolution, Newport never regained its prowess in the merchant trade, and only in 1847, with the advent of the Fall River line steamships, did Newport resume its role as a resort for southern and, later, New York tourists.

Just before and after the Civil War, Newport became a summer colony for artists and intellectuals, among them Henry James, Edith Wharton, William Wadsworth Longfellow (he wrote three poems about Newport), Edgar Allan Poe, Julia Ward Howe (who wrote "The Battle Hymn of the Republic") and Emma Lazarus (who wrote those words inscribed on the Statue of Liberty: "Give us your poor and huddled masses").

Newport's second Golden Age ran from the early 1880s until the 1929 Wall Street crash. It was the time when the "old rich" and the "new rich" of the American Industrial Age crowded aboard the Fall River line ferries from New York and Philadelphia to compete here on the battlefields of social power and prestige by building the most awesome European-style summer palaces and, in them, throwing the most extravagant and imaginative parties.

## Summer Home of the Gilded Age

Newport had become the summer home of the Gilded Age, the summer playground of the Astors, Belmonts, Vanderbilts and Goelets, where they played tennis, golf and polo and sailed their fabulous yachts. And they hired the best Beaux-Arts-style architects of the time—Richard Morris Hunt, Charles Follen McKim, Robert Swain Peabody, Horace Trumbauer, Stanford White Whitney Warren and John Russell Pope—to build their French-, Italian- and English-style multimillion-dollar villas and palaces, which they delighted in referring to as "summer cottages." (Hunt and Pope even built their own homes and studios here.)

Their summer party budgets were in the hundreds of thousands. On Sunday afternoons, these socialites climbed aboard their elegant horse-drawn carriages and, dressed in their best finery, paraded up and down Bellevue Avenue, their liveried footmen blowing their trumpets and dropping off calling cards at the mansions of their neighbors, who were never at home because they were out doing the same thing.

## The Sail Yachting Capital of New England

With its superb natural harbor, Newport is still the "Sail Yachting Capital of New England." It hosts annual jazz, folk and classical music festivals and national lawn tennis and croquet tournaments, and it's still a great swimming, hiking and watering place for young and old alike. (Rhode Island got its name because the explorer Giovanni da Verrazano thought it looked a bit like the Island of Rhodes, off the coast of Turkey.)

## Founded for Religious Freedom

Rhode Island was founded for religious freedom by Roger Williams in 1636, following his banishment from the Massachusetts Bay Colony because of his beliefs in the separation of church and state and religious tolerance.

In the Massachusetts Bay Colony, residents had religious freedom only for their own brand of Puritan state religion as determined by their religious leaders, who effectively ran the government.

After King Charles I's defeat by the Puritans, Williams returned to England in 1654 to have the patent reaffirmed by Cromwell's Parliament. After Charles II came to the throne in 1660, he sent John Clark back to England to obtain the Charter of 1663, which was ratified, after the American Revolution, as Rhode Island's state constitution until shortly before the Civil War. That charter called this state the "State of Rhode Island and Providence Plantations"—making the smallest state the one with the longest name!

Williams was a Calvinist and son of a London merchant tailor who had the very good fortune to get a solid education at Cambridge in England. There he became acquainted with John Winthrop, the Puritan leader who later became the first governor of the Massachusetts Bay Colony, and Oliver Cromwell, who later ruled England as Lord Protector and was perhaps the decisive force in the beheading of England's King Charles I.

## BOUGHT LAND FROM THE INDIANS

Roger Williams had the unusual notion that the colonists should actually buy their land from the Indians for fair value, as well as obtain a patent of charter from the English king. So in 1636, he purchased the land around the present city of Providence from the Narragansetts, called it Providence Plantations and, in 1643 and '44, returned to England to obtain a patent from the government of Charles I.

In 1638, just two years after Williams's banishment from the Bay Colony, some two hundred other religious dissidents involved in the Antinomian heresy and led by Anna Hutchinson were banished by the Massachusetts Bay Colony and founded the town of Pocasset, now called Portsmouth, on the north end of this island.

The Antinomians said that God could lead one to do things contrary to current laws or rules of church and state—an odd idea that can sometimes get one into trouble even today.

## Thirty Antinomians Founded Newport

Only a year later, in 1639, some thirty of those Antinomians, led by William Brenton, William Coddington and Nicholas Easton, moved to the south end of this island and founded Newport. And in that very first year, Brenton and Easton built wharves where Long Wharf now stands.

Many of these settlers had been wealthy landlords and merchants in England, and they brought their wealth and knowhow with them. And because Rhode Island offered religious tolerance, little practiced in the other colonies, Newport was soon flooded with Quakers, Anabaptists and other religious "deviators." In 1658, the first fifteen Sephardic Jewish families from the Island of Curacao sought refuge in Newport.

Many of the settlers were farmers, craftsmen, traders, housewrights and shipwrights, so they set to work building farms, workshops, shops, houses and ships. By 1741, it was reported that of the 120 Newport-owned ships in the harbor, almost all of them were made in Newport.

## Rum Traded for Slaves

Initially, trading was coastal trading with Boston, New York, Philadelphia, Charleston and ports in between. But by 1660, Newport also became involved in the very lucrative so-called triangular trade.

Rum distilled here in Newport was traded in the Guinea Gold Coast of Africa for slaves—often prisoners of war of the black warring African tribes—who were then traded to West Indies sugar plantation owners for their sugar and molasses, which were brought back to Newport to distill into rum.

Newport trade expanded so much over the next one hundred years that by 1760, its volume exceeded that of New York and had begun to rival that of Boston, Philadelphia and Charleston. Newport merchants were trading rice, flour, fish, whale oil, candles, lumber, fine crafted furniture and silver and rum. Newport was also one of the wealthiest trading cities, with many of its merchants venturing into smuggling, privateering (requiring a British license to raid and pirate French and Spanish ships) and outright piracy (requiring no license at all).

## GEORGE III CAME TO THE THRONE

In 1760, King George III came to the English throne. This was in the middle of the Seven Years' War—the British and Prussians against the French and Austrians. Here it was called the French and Indian War—the French colonists along the Mississippi and Ohio Valleys, the Great Lakes and Canada fighting the English colonies along the Atlantic coast.

But only two of our thirteen colonies met their home government's requisitions of men and money to fight the French colonists here, so England had to send mercenaries to help in the fighting. To cover these costs, Parliament began enforcing tariffs of the Trade and Navigation Acts, which had seldom been enforced before.

## SUGAR ACT CUTS INTO PROFITS

When the Seven Years' War ended in 1763, France ceded all of its Canadian and western lands to the British, except for New Orleans. Parliament thought the colonies would be pleased at the new prospects for expansion and should pay their fair share of the cost of the war, so in 1764 it imposed the Sugar Act. The sugar tax, as well as enforcement of the tariff on molasses, cut out much of the profit in the triangular trade.

Newporters were furious and responded by firing thirteen eighteen-pound cannon rounds from Fort George on Goat Island, damaging the British gunboat *St. John*, which had been pursuing smugglers. These were the first shots fired in opposition to the British authority by the colonists, but clashes continued over the next dozen years.

In 1765, passage of the Stamp Act, requiring a tax stamp on all legal documents and printed matter, including pamphlets, newspapers and even playing cards (used for gambling in the colonists' taverns), set off riots throughout the colonies. Here in Newport, windows were smashed in the houses of the tax collector and three prominent Tory sympathizers, who barely escaped with their lives and were hanged in effigy in front of the Colony House.

A boycott of British goods brought repeal of the Stamp Act, but it was replaced in 1767 by the Townshend Act, with taxes on glass, paint, lead, paper and tea (the English were drinking a lot of tea). There was another boycott and partial repeal. The Boston Massacre followed in 1770 and

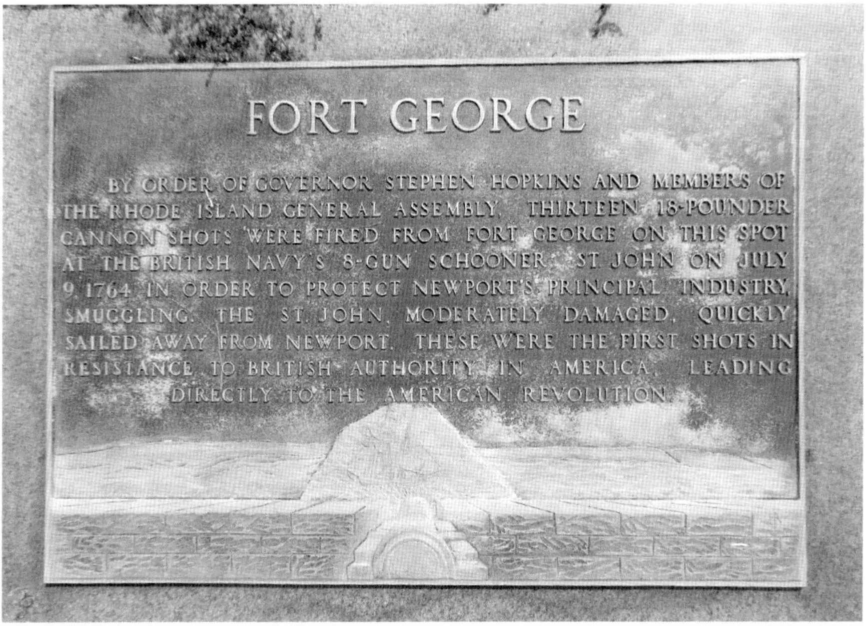


A bronze plaque commemorating the site of Fort George.

then, in 1772, the burning of the British gunboat *Gaspee* off the shore of Providence while it was pursuing a smuggler. The Boston Tea Party came in 1773—merchants, dressed as Indians, threw bales of tea off a British ship in protest to Parliament giving the British East India Company a monopoly in tea wholesaling. This undercut prices of smugglers and the colonial retailers here.

In 1774, Parliament responded to the Boston Tea Party by closing down the Port of Boston. In 1775, British troops fought colonists at Lexington and Concord while they were trying to capture rebel stores of gunpowder; at Bunker Hill, the British lost one thousand men—a third of their force—in winning the battle but convinced the colonists that they really were a match for British forces; and British gunboats blockaded Newport Harbor, closing it to all shipping.

## RHODE ISLANDERS FIRST TO DECLARE INDEPENDENCE

In 1776, it was all-out war. On May 4, from the balcony on the front of the Old Colony House, Rhode Island declared its independence from England—the first to declare—and the other twelve colonies declared two months later.

Because of stiff local resistance, the British withdrew their troops from Boston to Halifax. They defeated General George Washington on Long Island and took Manhattan. Britain's General Henry Clinton occupied Newport in December 1776 with six thousand men, who stayed here until November 1779. Meanwhile, there were battles at Princeton and Tiverton and the long winter at Valley Forge. The British occupied Philadelphia. But the surrender of Britain's General Burgoyne at Saratoga in 1779 finally convinced the French to openly side with the colonists. They sent troops and two fleets of gunboats.

Anticipating the French arrival, Clinton withdrew his troops in November 1779, concentrating his forces in New York and in efforts to subdue the southern colonies, where he expected less resistance.

## FRENCH TROOPS ARRIVED

Seven months later, in the summer of 1780, Admiral de Ternay arrived with forty-four ships and six thousand troops under the command of General de Rochambeau.

Newport's population of nine thousand, about one-third of them Tories, had withered to four thousand when Clinton withdrew. His troops had stripped the island of trees and then tore down more than 400 vacant houses of the 1,100 then in Newport just to burn the lumber as firewood.

## ROCHAMBEAU PERSUADES WASHINGTON

With the arrival of the French, many Tories fled, and Patriots returned. There was a great celebration of fireworks using cannon fire. The French stayed a year awaiting reinforcements. In March 1881, General Washington came here to map strategy with Comte Rochambeau, who persuaded

Washington to bypass General Cornwallis's southern forces, which had been withdrawn to Yorktown at the head of Chesapeake Bay.

The joint siege began in September. When a second French fleet from the West Indies confronted the British fleet unexpectedly, the British ships retreated to New York. Cornwallis's men surrendered a month later after running out of supplies.

Yorktown was the last major engagement of the war. Negotiations for peace dragged on for another eighteen months in Paris. In April 1883, the British agreed to grant the colonies independence. The treaty was signed in September.

*II*

# BIOGRAPHIES

## Commodore Matthew C. Perry

### *The Gracious U.S. Navy Man Who Did It All*

Though less flamboyant than his nine-years-older brother, Oliver Hazard Perry, who won the surrender of the British squadron of six ships on Lake Erie in 1813 and sent back the cryptic message "We have met the enemy and they are ours," Matthew Perry is credited as the founder of the U.S. Steamship Navy—instead of sailboats—and the opening of Japan to Western trade and the modern world.

Matthew joined the navy in 1809 at the age of fifteen. While serving on the frigate *President* during the war with England in 1812, he was promoted to acting lieutenant. Next, he served as second lieutenant aboard the brig *Chippewa* in fighting the Barbary pirates in 1819.

In 1817, the American Colonization Society was formed to emancipate American slaves and transport them to colonies in Africa. Matthew supported this idea and requested an appointment as first lieutenant on the USS *Cyanne* on the mission of escorting the first group of freed slaves to Africa in 1821.

His request was granted, so as first lieutenant on the USS *Cyanne*, he escorted the first group of freed slaves to Africa and there created for them the colony of Libya in 1821. In the 1820s, he again returned to hunting pirates in the West Indies aboard the vessel *Shark*. Next, he served as master commandant aboard the battleship *North Carolina*.

In 1833, Matthew won the position of captain of the Brooklyn Navy Yard and over the next ten years implemented navy reforms in recruiting, training and discipline that he had developed over the previous twenty years at sea.

In 1837, Perry wrote that the U.S. Navy had fallen to eighth place behind England and France and said that steam propulsion, iron hulls and shell guns were making sailing navies obsolete.

In the Brooklyn Navy Yard, he established an officers' lyceum, with weekly lectures for the instruction of young officers. And he was appointed in 1845 by Secretary of the Navy George Bancroft to prepare a better system of officer training; the end result, of course, was the U.S. Naval Academy at Annapolis.

(Coincidentally, Bancroft built the original Rosecliff cottage here on Bellevue Avenue and later sold it to Theresa Fair Oelrichs and her sister, Virginia Fair. The sisters later tore down that mansion and built the present Rosecliff, now owned by Newport's Preservation Society and open for tours.)

Then, Perry was back at sea in command of the African Squadron from 1843 to 1845. He became a key figure at Vera Cruz, in the Mexican War—his eight-inch guns opening holes in the city walls. Steamships and shell guns had shortened the siege significantly.

At age fifty-seven, Matthew was hoping for one more cruise before retirement, but in the wake of a treaty with China, there was new U.S. interest in opening trade with Japan, which had been completely isolated for over two centuries.

Unlike his glamorous, vivacious and daring older brother, Oliver, Matthew was patient, methodical and considerate of others—but equally determined to achieve his goals.

His mission to Japan included three main goals: 1) to arrange protection for American whaling ship seamen and property when wrecked on Japanese islands; 2) permission for American ships to enter one or more Japanese ports to obtain supplies in case of disaster or to refit and also to establish a depot for coal to refuel their ships; and 3) permission for American ships to enter one or more Japanese ports for purposes of trade.

Matthew arrived in a Japanese harbor on July 8, 1853, with four black ships sailing against the wind and with black smoke billowing out of their smokestacks—a sight the Japanese had never seen before.

Matthew knew enough about the failures of previous missions to Japan to realize he must first demonstrate respect for their customs and leaders by patience and diplomacy, since they looked on foreigners as barbarians.

Matthew's grandfather was a Quaker. Roger Williams had founded Rhode Island for religious freedom, and many early Newporters were Jews and Quakers. And just four years before this mission, he had welcomed the marriage of his daughter Caroline to the Jewish banker August Belmont.

When Japanese guard boats threw boarding ropes onto his ships upon his arrival, he cut the ropes. And he refused to leave until he had presented a letter from the U.S. president to a representative of the emperor of Japan. Otherwise, he said he would deliver the president's letter by force.

On July 14, representatives of the emperor finally received the letter, and Matthew told them he would return in the spring with a larger fleet of ships, bellowing black smoke, for the emperor's reply.

Matthew returned even earlier, in February 1854, with eight steamships bellowing black smoke. Negotiations resumed on March 8 in Yokohama. The emperor would supply American ships with fuel, water, provisions and coal and would treat shipwrecked sailors kindly. But no proposal to open Japan for foreign trade would be accepted, and Japan didn't need the profit.

However, the Japanese agreed to receive a copy of the recent treaty the United States had negotiated with China. Negotiations ended with the Treaty of Kanagawa, signed on March 31, 1854. It stated that any privilege granted to other nations would automatically be extended to the United States, and the U.S. Senate ratified the agreement unanimously.

In appreciation, the U.S. Congress granted Matthew $20,000 for acting "as a diplomatic envoy," and the governor and General Assembly of Rhode Island honored him in a ceremony in Newport's Colony House on June 15, 1855.

His statue in Newport's Touro Park was created by the sculptor John Quincy Adams Ward and its base by architect Richard Morris Hunt. It depicts events in the expedition to Japan, the Mexican War and the African liberation movement. This park is the site of the Black Ships Festival each July, in commemoration of Matthew Perry's expedition to Japan.

## August Belmont

### *Led New York High Society to Newport*

August Belmont was born to Jewish parents Simon and Frederika Schoenberg in Alzey, near Wiesbaden, Germany. After being apprenticed to the wealthy

Rothschild's Bank, he served it as a private secretary in Naples, Paris and Rome before arriving in New York at age twenty-three in 1837.

He discovered that the Rothschild's agents in New York had gone bankrupt, along with dozens of other financial firms, and had liabilities of $7 million.

August changed his name from the German "Schoenberg" to the French "Belmont," both meaning "beautiful mountain." Within three years, not only had he established Belmont & Company, American agent for the Rothschild's, but he was also one of the three most important private bankers in the United States.

In 1844, he was named counsel general of Austria in New York, and in 1849, he married Caroline Perry, daughter of Matthew Calbraith Perry, who returned from Japan in 1854 with the first treaty allowing American seamen to visit the port of Shimoda, ultimately opening Japan to Western trade.

From 1853 to 1857, Belmont served as U.S. minister to The Hague in Holland. Then, Belmont served as chairman of the National Democratic Party before and after the Civil War, and he dissuaded Rothschild's, and other bankers, from lending to the Confederacy.

Bythesea mansion, no longer standing. *Courtesy of the Redwood Library.*

In 1860, having found the Saratoga, New York resort "too commercial" and coming to Newport to visit Caroline's father, the Belmonts built their mansion, Bythesea, one of the early grand villas in Newport. They were the first to introduce ten-course dinners, with a staff of sixteen inside and ten outside dressed in full livery.

The Belmonts' Fifth Avenue mansion in New York also featured an art gallery with a glass-roofed dome supported by caryatid sculptures representing music, art, history and science to provide it with light.

In this New York mansion in 1860, the Belmonts entertained a team of twelve ambassadors from Japan, and in that year, Caroline lent her horse to the Prince of Wales (later England's Edward VII) for his triumphal entry into New York City.

When the Newport Casino's constitution and bylaws were adopted on June 11, 1880, August Belmont was elected president of the club; William A. Travers, who owned the Travers store block next door, was elected vice-president; and John N.A. Griswold, whose house is now the Newport Art Association Museum, was elected treasurer.

Belmont was also a famous horse breeder, first and longtime president of the American Jockey Club and the sponsor of the Belmont Jockey Horse Racing Cup in Jerome Park in the Bronx, New York. He died in 1890 at the age of seventy-seven.

## Alfred Smith

### *The Golden Goose Lays Gilded Eggs: Newport's Greatest Real Estate Developer*

Could a New York tailor transform Newport's fifty-year-old "real estate hangover," which followed the American Revolution, into the most fashionable watering place of New York's Gilded Age high society?

Many say Newport native son Alfred Smith did just that during his forty-one-year-long real estate career here. It included playing a major role not only in building Bellevue, Wellington, Harrison and Ocean Avenues but also in the development of the Kay, Catherine and Old Beach Road areas and rebuilding Bath Road (now called Memorial Boulevard) down to Eaton's Farm and Beach.

A poor boy whose ancestor Edward Smith is said to have helped John Clark secure Rhode Island's 1663 Royal Charter from England's King Charles II, Alfred was born in 1808 on the street now called Aquidneck Avenue, according to Alan T. Schumacher's biographical sketch printed in the Newport Historical Society's *Spring Bulletin* of 1988.

When Alfred's family abandoned farming in Middletown after he received a rudimentary district school education, they moved to Newport's Cross Street, near The Point, and apprenticed him as a tailor to the Quaker firm of Isaac Gould & Son.

Under Gould's apprenticeship rules, Alfred could not drink, gamble, remain in bed after sunrise "or otherwise sin." Skill and thrift led to a brief stint as a cloth cutter in Providence, and then it was on to New York City's fashionable tailors Wheeler & Co. on Broadway. There, he was soon earning the very considerable sum of $6,000 a year from extremely wealthy clients.

Tiring of New York City's fast-paced life and still hungering for his love of gardening, Alfred returned in 1839 at the age of thirty to his native Newport with thrift-induced savings of $20,000 to launch himself on a new career.

But first things first. In February 1843, Smith married Anna Maria, the daughter of Captain Allen Talbot. His son Howard was born the next year, during which Smith bought land on Mount Vernon Street. A house at number twelve and a greenhouse and gardens appeared on the land the next year, and then three daughters were born to the couple.

The handsome Greek Revival–style house, now condominiums, still stands, and for many years the house also served as Smith's real estate office. Exotic trees and flowers from Europe were grown in his gardens and praised by the local weekly newspaper, the *Newport Mercury*, as early as 1850 as "the finest in the state."

Just four years before leaving the tailoring trade in New York, Smith had already interested one of his wealthy and influential sartorial customers, William Beach Lawrence, in buying the sixty-acre Ochre Point Farm here in Newport for $12,000 as a real estate investment.

An authority on international law and later lieutenant governor of Rhode Island, Lawrence discovered Smith's advice was truly prescient. This farm, research suggests, included a strip along the shore to the east of Ochre Point Avenue but also to the west of it as far as Lawrence Avenue and south of Webster Street as far as the shore. Today, it is the site of five of Newport's most spectacular mansions: the Breakers, Vinland, Ochre Court, Anglesea and Fairholme.

The house built by Alfred Smith, the "golden goose that laid gilded eggs," after returning to his native Newport with his $20,000 tailor's earnings and before he launched his fabulous Newport real estate career.

With this canny knack for real estate development, coupled with his interest in trees and landscape architecture, in 1845 Smith formed a syndicate with two others and bought three hundred acres to the east and south of the present site of the Viking Hotel on Touro Street (now Bellevue Avenue) and turned it into a grid of tree-lined lots.

Smith's timing was perfect. The Greek Revival Atlantic House Hotel (now the site of the Elks Lodge) had opened the previous year. The six-hundred-bed Ocean House (now the site of the Bellevue Shopping Plaza) was opened in 1847. Those floating palaces propelled by paddle wheels—the Fall River line steamships—were just starting to link on their overnight runs to New York, and many books and periodicals suddenly began touting Newport's scenic, climatic and recreational virtues, which later in the Gilded Age would win Newport the title of the "Queen of Resorts."

The 11,000 Newport residents before the American Revolution had dwindled to 4,500 during the three-year occupation by some 6,000 British troops. By 1790, the number of residents had risen to only 6,716, and by

1840, the population was just 8,334. From being the country's fifth-ranking Atlantic seaport and a cool haven for southern plantation owners, Newport's recovery was painfully slow.

A series of travel guides reciting a litany of Newport's climate, scenery and early colonial and Revolutionary War history was sparked as early as 1840 by Sarah Calhoone's *A Week in Newport*. She closes it with this quote from our second president, John Adams: "Newport is the loveliest gem on the bosom of the sea."

At first, the returning southern tourists rented boardinghouses. But as early as 1839, the largest plantation owner in Savannah, Georgia, George Noble Jones, hired English architect Richard Upjohn to build the substantial Gothic Revival–style mansion (since renamed Kingscote) at the corner of West Bowery and Bellevue.

In 1852, *A Handbook of Newport and Rhode Island* by George Phillips (pen name for Ross Dix) compared Newport's climate to that of England's Isle of Wight and called our island a "Garden of Eden." The book contains a series of stories about the Viking Tower in Touro Park as immortalized in a Longfellow poem; the wonders of Purgatory Chasm, Hanging Rock, the Forty Steps "of wood," Coggeshall Ledge, the Atlantic and Ocean House Hotels, Dr. George Berkeley and Whitehall; and the capture of Revolutionary War British general William Prescott, the Lilly Pond, Spouting Rock and War of 1812 navy hero Oliver Hazard Perry.

It also included a list of physicians, lawyers, banks, newspapers and hotels. Among the latter were Belle Vue Hotel, "with a dining room," on Catherine Street; the U.S. Hotel; the Park House; the Pelham Street House; and five boardinghouses, including Bateman's House on Castle Hill. It also praised the Germania Musical Society's concerts.

Also in 1852, George W. Curtis published *Lotus Eating: A Summer Book* extolling Newport as the "greatest watering place in the country," and it contained a litany of attractions. And again, two years later, *Newport Mercury* editor and artist George Champlain Mason published a series of drawings that dramatized its scenic attractions.

Newport's tailor turned real estate promoter was not sleeping through this barrage of books, as well as periodicals, about Newport. In 1851, Smith formed a partnership with his friend Joseph I. Bailey, who had inherited and otherwise acquired 140 acres in the area of Bailey's Beach, popular for saltwater bathing. This was at a time when Bailey's other family members were moving to San Francisco.

Bailey, who put up $27,00 (and Smith probably an equal amount), expressed doubts about the financial prospects, saying, "All I expected to get out of the bargain is driftwood enough to keep me warm in the winter."

But the following year, through Smith's persuasion of the town council (and later thirty adjacent property owners), construction of the fifty-foot-wide Bellevue Avenue was begun. And by the time it was finished in 1853, Smith had planted hundreds of trees along it.

The year 1853 was a very good one for Newport. The Newport Gas Co. was incorporated, the Newport Reading Room and the Newport Historical Society were founded and the Newport Township was reincorporated as a city.

And in the winter of 1853–54, sixty new houses were built here, real estate values had tripled and Smith was the seventh-wealthiest man in Newport, according to tax records.

Prior to 1852, Bellevue Street (apparently named after the Belle Vue Hotel) had extended from Tour at Kay Street to just beyond Narragansett Avenue, where, in 1848, Albert Sumner had built his Rockery Hall. Smith extended Bellevue to Spouting Horn, a Bailey's Beach rock formation that, at very high tides, sent a water spout as high as thirty feet in the air.

There was no rest for Smith. In 1856, a subscription was raised largely through Smith's efforts, and Bath Road, now called Memorial Boulevard, was rebuilt down to Easton's Farm and Beach—popular for saltwater swimming, then considered to have healthful benefits.

Being a smart real estate developer, when selling the Bellevue Avenue lots Smith always included in the deed the right to use a swimming pavilion at Spouting Horn—now called Spouting Rock Beach Association or Bailey's Beach—which some still claim to be one of the world's most exclusive. Those not having a deeded right to use the swimming pavilion paid a daily or seasonal fee, providing revenue to Smith, Bailey and their heirs until it was finally sold for a private club in 1897.

On the advice of realtor Smith in 1857, Edward King purchased the Harrison Farm on the south side of Newport Harbor and deeded to the city the land on which Harrison and Wellington Avenues were built, replacing a rutty dirt track to Fort Adams and Castle Hill.

Smith's initiative to link Harrison Avenue by a shore road to Bellevue Avenue was interrupted by the Civil War. But after Smith himself paid to put up a stone bridge over the creek that ran from Almy Pond to Bailey's Beach, Ocean Avenue was finally completed in 1867.

The new southern shore road provided a scenic horse and carriage ride almost as spectacular as that on Cliff Walk—and you didn't have to get out of your buggy to see it.

In 1852, the tax records listed only a dozen summer colonists owning real estate here, but in 1875, *Newport Mercury* editor turned architect George Champlin Mason published his illustrated tome, "Newport and Its Cottages," with full-page engravings showing forty-two elegant mansions, more than half of them owned by New Yorkers. And one of them, Bythesea, was built by Mason himself for August Belmont, who had founded the New York branch of the Rothschild's Bank and had married one of the daughters of Matthew Perry.

But in 1875, there were actually about five hundred cottages here, and a good proportion of them were available for rent for up to $2,000 to $5,000 for the summer season. In the same year, Newport's population stood at over twelve thousand. By 1885, it had risen to nearly twenty thousand.

Smith's realty sales ranged across large areas of Newport and Middletown, and in 1872 alone, he rented 106 furnished homes for $464,000.

Smith's business terms were exact. He paid promptly and demanded prompt payment of debts owed him. He lent money for real estate purposes at 7.3 percent, which earned him an even two cents a day on a $100 debt, simplifying his bookkeeping.

During his forty-one-year real estate career, Smith had combined total sales of $21 million, and upon his death in 1886, he left an estate of just under $2 million. Not too bad for an obscure tailor who had returned to his native town with savings of $20,000 and launched himself on a new career

People used to say that if Smith got you in his carriage, he wouldn't let you out until you bought some property. But they also said he wouldn't sell a property unless the buyer had previously been approved by neighboring property owners—an illegal practice today known as "steering."

By 1874, *Harper's* magazine was heralding Smith as "the chief of real estate agents in Newport, nearly all of the transactions of the vicinity being made through him or his firm, Alfred Smith and Son."

At times, Smith mixed generosity with business acumen. In 1865, when the Redwood Library needed more land, Smith donated $500 toward the purchase price of $15,000 for the adjacent lot, but he also collected a commission on that sale.

Later, Smith gave a chime of nine bells—the largest of which weighed in at three thousand pounds—for the Channing Memorial Unitarian Church at Touro Park. His wife, Anna Maria Talbot Smith, was an ardent member and was beloved by the whole community. She died at age sixty-four on February 28, 1884.

A modest person, Anna was known for her charitable deeds, and like her husband of forty-one years, she was untouched by the high life of Newport's summer cottagers. Her funeral in the Channing church was very large and filled to overflowing with many mourners.

The memorial to her in the Island Cemetery shows an angelic figure, carved in relief by the sculptor Augustus Saint-Gaudens. And it bears the inscription: "For they rest from their labors and their works do follow them."

In October of the very next year, Smith was stricken with a paralytic stroke on the right side, which also affected his mind. One of his son-in-laws, Colonel A. Prescott Baker of Boston, was appointed guardian of his estate, which included about $376,570 in real estate and $1,610,358 in personal property—mainly in tax-exempt government bonds and National Bank stock, according to the appraisal.

It was in the very same month of October, in the very same year of 1885, on the twelfth day of that month, that Pierre Lorillard deeded The Breakers to Cornelius Vanderbilt II. The mortgage holder, in the amount of $80,000 in the transaction, was none other than Alfred Smith.

Smith had guaranteed the original mortgage in the amount of $90,000.00 when Lorillard bought the thirteen-acre site from Governor William Beach Lawrence on August 28, 1877, at a price of $96,147.83. The following year, Lorillard hired the Boston architects Peabody and Sterns to build the original Breakers at a cost of $90,000.00. (That first Breakers, sold to Vanderbilt in 1885, burned to the ground in 1892, at which time Vanderbilt hired architect Richard Morris Hunt to build the new Breakers, which still stands on the site.)

On November 28, 1879, Smith, as guarantor, had assumed the Lawrence mortgage, which by then had been reduced to $80,000. On November 12, 1885, only a month after buying The Breakers from Lorillard, and roughly a month after Smith had suffered his paralytic stroke, Cornelius Vanderbilt paid off in full the $80,000 balance to Smith's guardian, Colonel Baker.

That thirteen-acre lot on which The Breakers stands was part of the sixty-acre Ochre Point Farm Alfred Smith had so wisely counseled William Beach Lawrence to buy for $12,000 in 1835—just four years before Smith gave up the tailoring trade in New York to launch his real estate career in Newport.

But could Smith have shown such sparkling success without those Fall River line overnight steamship links to New York or without that avalanche of publicity led in part by *Newport Mercury* editor turned architect George Champlin Mason, who knew how to give voice to his praises of this town as follows:

> *The natural attractions of Newport are great. But it does not depend on these alone to engage the attraction of strangers who would while away a few summer days by the shore.*
>
> *On every hand are beautiful county seats of every known and unknown order of architecture; numerous hotels and all well conducted; libraries of well stored and well selected books, easy of access; society composed of leading men of the country, in all the walks of life; stately matrons and dashing bells—all combine their attractions; and serve to make Newport the most desirable and popular of resorts.*

Who could resist that paean of praise?

Just a year after his paralytic stroke, on October 26, 1886, Smith died, leaving no will and four grown children. His son-in-law, Colonel Baker, administered his estate. A month later, his house cum office at 12 Mount Vernon Street, including the greenhouse and gardens, went to his son Howard, who continued in the real estate business. The office had been moved to the Muenchinger Building, at 57 Bellevue Avenue, a few years before. Howard died in Palm Beach in 1901.

*This account is based in part on Alan T. Schumacher's biographical report printed in the Newport Historical Society's* Spring Bulletin *of 1988, which includes research by the society's librarian, Bertram Lippincott III.*

## JAMES G. BENNETT

### *Shy about Marriage, Builds Newport Casino, Center of Newport Social Life*

Unable to control outrageous impulses, James Gordon Bennett Jr. won the first transatlantic yachting race, was a founder of the American Jockey Club, singlehandedly introduced the sport of polo to the United States, fought the last gentleman's duel in the United States, was ostracized from New York high society for life and predicted his own death within four days.

Born rich to a father who founded the *New York Herald* newspaper as a one-cent-an-issue tabloid and was frequently horsewhipped for exposing financial swindles and for daring to use the unmentionable word "petticoat" in his crime and society columns, James Gordon Bennett Jr. was spoiled from birth by his mother, who chose to bring him up in Paris because she couldn't stand the filthy, irreverent abuse continuously leveled at her vociferous husband.

James Jr. was born on May 10, 1841, at 114 Chambers Street in Lower New York when his father was forty-six and his mother was twenty-four—just one year after their marriage. That felicitous event had been greeted by rival editors of the *New York Herald* with both insidious slander and abuse.

James Sr. had long been subjected to such abuse from his rival newspaper editors, as well as readers, but his bride, Henriette Agnes Crean, was gentle and unprepared, even nine years later, when her husband was horsewhipped in her presence by New York district attorney candidate John Graham (and two of Graham's brothers) because of the *New York Herald*'s role in defeating his candidacy. All the while, two policemen watched the violence without interfering.

Then, two years later, black gunpowder was seen leaking from a package delivered to the *Herald* offices. Police wetted down the package and discovered that, if opened, it would have blown the publisher and staff to smithereens.

That was finally enough to convince Mrs. Bennett to take James Jr. and his younger sister, Jeannette, to Paris and salubrious accommodations with housemaids and tutors to bring them up in the style that the owner of the *New York Herald* was now able to afford.

James Gordon Bennett Sr. was born near Keath in Banffshire, Scotland, in 1795. He was educated in the Roman Catholic Seminary in Aberdeen, but in 1819, at the age of twenty-four, he immigrated to Halifax, Nova Scotia, and then to Boston, New York and Charleston, South Carolina, working variously as a teacher, proofreader, lecturer on political economy, copyeditor and Tammany Hall Democratic Party ward healer.

In New York over the next ten years, he worked for various journals, serving as Washington correspondent of the *New York Enquirer* and associate editor of the combined *Courier and Enquirer*.

In 1832, he founded the short-lived *Globe*. In 1833–34, he was chief editor of the *Pennsylvanian* in Philadelphia. Then, on May 6, 1835, with capital of $500 from a basement at 20 Wall Street, he printed the first edition of the *New York Herald*. At one cent a copy, it was aimed squarely at the working class.

"We shall support no party, be the organ of no political faction or coterie and care nothing for any election of candidate from president down to constable," he pledged. "We shall endeavor to record facts on every public and proper subject, stripped from verbiage and coloring, with comments, when suitable—just, independent and fearless."

Outspoken from the first, Bennett said, "I shall mix together commerce and business, pure religion and morals, literature and poetry, the drama and dramatic purity, till the *Herald* shall outstrip everything in the conception of man."

He announced the function of a newspaper was "not to instruct but to startle." One might interpret that word more broadly today to mean "to astonish, to arouse or to shock!"

Previously, newspapers were mainly editorials expressing the views of the publisher. On June 13, 1835, the *Herald* printed the first Wall Street financial article to appear in any U.S. newspaper. In December, a story about a great fire in the city, including both an illustration and a map showing the damaged areas, appeared. Real factual news—how astonishing!

On April 12, 1836, Bennett reported a hatchet murder of a playgirl named Ellen Jewett in a brothel in Thomas Street in full gory detail. Other newspapers reported such events, if at all, in a few brief sentences. Bennett visited the crime scene and disclosed that the chief suspect, Richard P. Robinson, was accused solely because he had left his cloak at the scene while visiting the girl earlier in the evening.

With no other evidence against him, Robinson was eventually acquitted, but Bennett was accused by other New York journals of taking a bribe to suppress other evidence. The effect of the controversy boosted the *Herald*'s circulation from five thousand to fifteen thousand a day.

In 1838, Bennett hired the first European correspondent for an American newspaper. With the development of the steamship service across the Atlantic and the development of the telegraph, Bennett was quick to adopt use of these services, widening Americans' understanding of the world. He began reporting social news with somewhat satirical comments, offending the rich and delighting the poor. And truly unsettling indeed was the *Herald*'s innovation of publishing a list of bankruptcies. How awful. Horsewhip the wretch, for God's sake!

Then came Bennett's campaign against prudery, which really shook up the bluenoses and new puritans. In a May issue of the *Herald* in 1840, he rallied against calling arms and legs "branches of the body"; trousers, "inexpressibles"; shirts, "linens"; and petticoats, unmentionable "unmentionables."

"Petticoats, petticoats, petticoats, vent your mawkishness on that," he taunted in his editorial.

Bluebloods and editorialists of other newspapers cried, "Outrage! Ban the *Herald* from being sold in your hotels and clubs and on street corners!" But one month later, the *Herald* printed a table showing other New York press organs had a combined circulation of only thirty-six thousand when the *Herald*'s had risen to fifty-one thousand.

Bennett had a genius for playing popular causes to his own benefit, which he did in the case of suffragettes. Their cause of voting rights for women was generally unpopular at the time, especially among males, who were the largest group buying newspapers.

"Motherhood was the best cure for the mania," Bennett proclaimed and suggested that the cause's leaders would eventually return to their rightful place in the kitchen.

Though Bennett's *New York Herald* was soon making millions, he himself always remained an outsider—politically, socially and privately—even after his marriage to that sweet, beautiful Irish girl Henrietta Crean. And though he lavished thousands of dollars on her and the care of their two children, and even went occasionally for short visits to see them in Paris, his real passion was always the *New York Herald*, day and night, and how to make it more popular and profitable.

James Jr.'s every whim had been satisfied and coddled from the cradle onward, and he grew to be tall, aristocratic in bearing, haughty and beaked nosed, with dark, darting, suspicious blue eyes. He was demanding, arrogant and, most surprisingly, able to hold his own in a fistfight.

He was also eloquently well tutored in the French language and in horseback riding, and one of his French tutors had introduced him to the pleasures of alcohol and intimacies with the opposite sex shortly after he reached the age of puberty.

During his lengthening visits to New York, his stern and rather cautious father first bought James Jr. a trim sailing sloop, the *Rebecca*. He then bought his son the 160-ton yacht *Henrietta*, named after his mother. He also hired a renowned sea dog, Captain Samuel "Bulley" Samuels, to take charge of the vessel in hopes that Samuels could teach Junior some seagoing discipline.

Samuels was not totally without success. In 1857, at the age of sixteen, James Jr. was elected to membership in the prestigious New York Yacht Club—something his acrimonious father could never have hoped to achieve.

When the Civil War broke out in 1861, James Jr. acquired a sudden longing for naval glory, so the doting James Sr. sent his legal representative to open negotiations with President Abraham Lincoln. The *Herald* would enthusiastically back the Union cause, and James Jr. would become a third lieutenant on his own yacht, the *Henrietta*, in the Union's Revenue Cutter Service.

The *Henrietta* was commissioned and equipped with three six-pound brass cannons and joined a blockading squadron off Point Royal, South Carolina. In under a year, the Union navy decommissioned the *Henrietta*, and James Jr. tendered his resignation on May 11, 1862, without explanation. He returned to his regular apprenticeship at the *Herald*, begun when he was a teenager.

In his office, James Sr. had installed two desks, one on either side of his own. One was for his son and the other for Edward Townsend Flynn. Flynn was an office boy whom James Sr. had promoted to be companion, coworker and friend to James Jr., with the hope that he could inspire responsibility and keep Junior out of trouble during his frequent bouts of arrogance and with alcohol.

Flynn had a very delicate assignment, indeed. After a morning in his father's office, James Jr. often developed a considerable thirst for champagne. One day, in Delmonico's Restaurant, James Jr. spilled some customers' drinks as he charged to the bar to complain about a fifteen-minute wait. When a young customer asked if he had ordered a whole case, Junior's fist missed the guy's chin. Instead, the young man knocked James Jr. unconscious with a single blow to the jaw.

Later, to avoid complications, Flynn claimed to James Sr. that he had been called away before the incident took place. When James Jr. learned that the young customer was a well-known prizefighter, Billy Edwards, he accepted the humiliation gladly and made Edwards his best friend.

James Jr.'s acceptance into the Gilded Age fashionable world—so unlike his father's world of hard work—was led by the wealthy Leonard Jerome, who liked Junior's flair for riding his road coach and horses, dressed in high fashion, at high speed around New York City's most fashionable neighborhoods.

A true gallant! His unsociable father had already made the *New York Herald* the most prosperous newspaper in America. Junior couldn't just sit and watch his father run things. But when James Jr.'s wild coach driving almost took the life of Jerome's daughter Jennie, it came very close to altering British history. She escaped injury in the crash and later married Lord Randolph Churchill; one of their sons was Winston Churchill.

Leonard Jerome established a racetrack called Jerome Park on an old estate at Fordham in the Bronx and organized the first meeting of the New York

Jockey Club in September 1866. Among members at that first meeting were the German-born banker August Belmont; Boss William Tweed, headman of Tammany Hall; Lieutenant General Ulysses S. Grant; and James Gordon Bennett Jr.

Only ten years later, in 1876, Bennett, like Jerome, became a great innovator by almost single-handedly introducing the sport of polo to the United States. Officers of the Indian army had brought the sport of polo to England, and Bennett, while on a visit there, became so enthralled by it that he got one of the officers, Captain Henry Augustus "Sugar" Candy, a retired officer of the queen's Ninth Royal Lancers, to come to America to teach his wealthy fellow New Yorkers—men like August Belmont, William P. Douglas and Frank Gray—how to play. They began holding polo matches after the horse races at Jerome Park and then founded the Westchester Polo Club, built a clubhouse and hired one of the Delmonico's cooks to orchestrate their cuisine.

So at age twenty-five, James Jr. was literally the founder of American polo.

And James Jr.'s career as the greatest newspaperman of his generation was really launched from the deck of his yacht, *Henrietta*, on Christmas Day 1866, when he won a perilous 3,106-mile transatlantic ocean race to Cowes Roads, on the coast of England, in only thirteen days, twenty-one hours and fifty-five minutes.

Bennett's pilot, the old seadog "Bulley" Samuels, won him the victory over the *Fleetwing*, owned by George Osgood (eight hours, fifteen minutes later) and the *Vestia*, owned by Pierre Lorillard (forty minutes after Osgood).

The idea of the race was born over cigars and brandy at the New York's prestigious Union Club.

James Sr. was so proud of his son's sensational victory in the stormy December ocean waves that he immediately granted him control of the *New York Herald* newspaper—and just a year later, the New York Yacht Club promoted James Jr. to be its commodore.

The new commodore immediately began reporting to work on time in an elaborately decorated horse-drawn carriage, elegantly dressed with a drooping, well-trimmed mustache.

"I'm the only one to be pleased," he announced to his startled elderly newspaper staff. "If I want the *Herald* to be turned upside down, it shall be turned upside down!"

And after only a few short months on the job, in July 1887, young Bennett came out with a new, spicier afternoon edition of the paper called the *Evening Telegram*. It was printed on pink paper with four six-column pages at only one cent a copy.

It printed the more radical sensational stuff, like his father's original *Herald* news presentation, which over the years had developed an appeal to the wealthier educated class—no more expecting women to return to their rightful place in the kitchen or to forget about divorce.

The sight of Junior's new *Evening Telegram* reassured James Sr. that his son was getting a grasp on real journalism. But when, two months later, James Jr. changed the *Herald* masthead to read "Jr." instead of "Sr." as editor in chief and publisher, the elder Bennett stopped the presses.

The old masthead was restored, and James Sr. told his son, "I'm not retiring till I'm good and ready!"

But on New Years Day 1868 at the *Herald* offices, the seventy-three-year-old father turned over ownership papers for both papers to his twenty-six-year-old son without any ceremony.

The elderly reporting staff found their new boss difficult to please yet equally innovative and impulsive. He intended to make news, not just report it, and footing the bill would be expensive. He was ready to pay as well as innovate.

He employed the newly perfected transatlantic cable, at tolls mounting to $7,000 in gold, to report the king of Prussia's peace terms with Austria. He paid $3,000 in telegraph tolls when his reporter sent a fifty-thousand-word account of the massacre in General Custer's Last Stand at Little Bighorn.

The *Herald*'s report beat the competing newspapers by four days. Young Bennett followed his father's dictum: the purpose of the newspaper was not to educate but to startle.

The *Herald* was making $750,000 a year, averaging sixty thousand copies daily at five cents a copy. The *New York Times* and the *Tribune* were selling at four cents on eight pages. But the *Herald* ran to twelve pages.

Among literary figures hired as regular contributors by the young owner were Mark Twain and Walt Whitman. But perhaps James Jr.'s greatest triumph resulted in 1869 from hiring the rugged Henry M. Stanley to find the long-lost missionary Dr. David Livingston in the jungles of Central Africa.

With an armed escort of 34 men, 143 porters and twenty-seven pack animals, the relentless Stanley struggled for eight months along the Arab caravan route to Lake Tanganyika. He faced mutiny, desertions, illness and fever from his crew. But outside Hiji on the shore of Lake Tanganyika, he approached a white man, saying, "Dr. Livingston, I presume?" And it was Livingston, replying he'd "never been lost" during his five years of African wanderings.

Stanley became almost as famous as Livingston, and from the cable dispatches about Stanley's journey, the *Herald* newspaper circulation rose to 100,000 a day. Bennett was pleased as punch until Stanley's fame began outstripping his own.

Later, Stanley explored the entire African Congo River delta for Bennett, and another rugged reporter also explored the steppes of Central Asia for him. Newsreaders were learning about the world.

On June 1, 1872, at the age of seventy-seven, James Gordon Bennett Sr. suffered a stroke and died within hours. It was just over four years after he had turned over control of the *Herald* and *Evening Telegram* to his son and just months after his years-younger wife and his daughter, Jeanette, had come from Paris to New York for a month-long visit.

It was in the summer of 1875 that James Jr. began taking on a new view of the world by courting the beautiful Miss Caroline May. His numerous romances from his youth in Paris onward had never remotely approached the church altar. Perhaps the *Herald*'s news coverage of one of New York's leading law firms was a contributing deterrent to breach of promise lawsuits.

Caroline's father, Dr. William May, and her mother, brothers and cousins became frequent guests at Bennett's grand mansion, Stone Villa, on Newport, Rhode Island's Bellevue Avenue before Bennett announced his engagement to Caroline.

On the late afternoon of New Year's Day 1877, Bennett arrived, somewhat intoxicated, with his coachman at the May home on New York's West Nineteenth Street to celebrate his engagement to the radiant Caroline.

With his usual verbose bravado, the commodore made his rounds of the imbibing guests, cracking bawdy jokes and slapping some of his personal friends on the back. But upon approaching the blazing drawing room fireplace and remembering his lifetime motto to never resist an impulse, he announced, "There's no bathroom within half a block!" Opening his pants, he urinated directly into the sputtering fire.

The ladies screamed and rushed to the maids for their coats. Two of Bennett's own friends took him firmly by each arm and dashed him out the Mays' front door to Bennett's coachman and sleigh, with orders to take him to his townhouse and put him to bed.

Bennett woke the next day with a blistering hangover. For Bennett, apologizing to Caroline and her entire family and friends—he, the commodore of the New York Yacht Club since age seventeen and the publisher of the most powerful newspaper in the United States—was not a foregone conclusion.

He dressed and trotted down to New York's Union Club, where fellow members received him with polite and curious stares. With the absence of a swift apology from her fiancé, Caroline had no choice but to send a note saying their engagement was terminated.

After a full luncheon at the club, Bennett headed straight for the *Herald*'s office. But Caroline's brother met him outside with a long cowhide whip like the one that had been used on Bennett's father in the early publishing days of the *Herald*.

The thongs of the whip drew blood from Bennett's neck, and the two men rolled in the snow. They punched each other until the club members pulled them apart.

Even though all the rival newspapers in New York had a field day over the whole incident, the *Herald* was silent. Instead, Bennett sent emissaries challenging Fred May to a pistol duel at twelve paces at Slaughters Gap, on the border between Maryland and Delaware, at 2:00 p.m. on the afternoon of January 7.

The challenge was delivered by Charles Longfellow, the poet's son, who had accompanied Bennett on the *Henrietta*'s race across the Atlantic. Both men arrived on time with their seconds, took twelve paces and opened fire in the air. No blood flowed.

Since Bennett was a first-class shot, there had surely been a profession of good will. The two men then ordered beer at the local Dover Hotel and shook hands.

Bennett was still welcome at the Union Club and among gentlemen friends, but not by Fifth Avenue hostesses at mixed gatherings, as they would certainly make sure he was not given the opportunity to pee in their own fireplaces. "Horrors, no!"

A lonely bachelor with no women to cultivate? Folks were much more forgiving of human frailties in Paris, where Bennett had been brought up. Why not Paris, indeed?

Soon after his self-imposed exile in Paris in 1878, Bennett, for several days, drove his carriage through the grand boulevards with a donkey inside it.

"This donkey is the most sensible American in Paris," said a sign he hung on the donkey's neck. It was the *Herald* newspaper publisher's way of distinguishing himself from the orthodox thinking of many of his American countrymen.

Bennett acquired four grand French residences, one at number 120 on the Champs Elysees. By cable from Paris, Commodore Bennett commanded and edited the *Herald* and the *Evening Telegram*. His revolving door of editors, correspondents, managers and reporters continued to keep all of them on their toes, as did his infrequent surprise appearances in the New York offices of the *Herald* on Park Row.

After one of these surprise New York visits in 1779 with his old polo-playing buddy Captain Henry Augustus "Sugar" Candy, he traveled on to his Newport, Rhode Island Bellevue Avenue mansion, Stone Villa.

And after enjoying a polo practice session on Izzard's Field (now known as Morton's Park), Bennett and Candy rode their polo ponies down Bellevue to the exclusive Newport Reading Room, the private men's club founded in 1853, for some liquid refreshment.

Strongly anticipating the drink, Bennett challenged Candy to ride his pony through the club's front door.

Candy did it, but the club members were not amused by the stunt. They censured Bennett and stripped Candy of his temporary membership in the club. The commodore's response? "I'll build my own club!"

Bennett hired the nascent architectural firm of McKim, Mead and White for the job and called the new club the Newport Casino. With its horse and flower shows, its horseshoe piazza for viewing, its lawn and court tennis tournaments, its balls and theater, its reading and dining rooms, its card and billiard rooms and its club rooms and bachelors' quarters, it came to serve as a pattern for similar clubs across the country.

The architects Charles McKim and Stanford White introduced a variety of patterned cedar shingles in the casino design. They developed the design after a tour of New England's old colonial buildings. It came to subsequently be known as the Shingle style, and the casino became the center of Newport's social life. Bennett was more than welcome in Newport but soon after returned with his friend Candy to Paris.

Then, on October 8, 1887, he launched the first edition of the *Paris Herald* newspaper. It was full of news about American, French and other European socialites and politics. It was, in fact, a fresh breeze compared to the traditional continental newspapers. It was an international society sheet with stories on the best places to eat but also about a jewel thief in Berlin, the death of a Russian lady attributed to a tight corset and whether waltzing is really wicked.

Transatlantic cable rate price wars broke out between Jay Gould, Clarence McKay and Bennett. The *Paris Herald* was a clever mix of news and gossip. It was a new sport for the commodore of the New York Yacht Club to play in Paris.

The commodore also noted that New York society was moving uptown to mid-Manhattan. In the newspaper circulation wars, he had been battling Joseph Pulitzer and William Randolph Hearst. Pulitzer was building a fourteen-story golden-domed skyscraper near the Brooklyn Bridge, which Bennett considered "bad taste."

Commodore Bennett would move the *Herald* from Park Row at Ann Street and Broadway to what has ever since been called Herald Square. It is still at the intersection of Thirty-fifth Street, Broadway and Sixth Avenue. The new Herald Building was to be modeled after the Doge's Palace in Venice, Italy.

Bennett chose Stanford White, the junior partner of McKim, Mead and White, to design a building reflecting the eminence of the *New York Herald* and its owner in the world of publishing.

White thought Venice's Doge's Palace a little too grand and argued that the Palazzo del Consiglio in Verona might be more appropriate as a prototype. Uncharacteristically, Bennett backed down but never recaptured his initial enthusiasm.

The magnificent two-story arcade was supported by columns on three sides; the fourth side's glass windows showed the presses rolling out as many as ninety thousand copies of the *Herald* every hour.

At Bennett's insistence, the roof line was decorated with twenty-six four-foot-tall bronze statues of owls—Bennett's favorite symbol—on three-foot-high pedestal bases, each with flashing electric light bulbs for eyes, symbolizing the wisdom going into the printed pages of the *New York Herald.*

Also standing on the roof was a statue of Minerva, goddess of wisdom, and below her was a bell and two bell ringer figures, representing typesetters, who would strike the bell on the hour with hammers to let New Yorkers know the time of day. They were known humorously as "Stuff and Guff."

On being reminded by his manager that he held only a thirty-year lease on the Herald Square building site, Bennett said, "Thirty years from now the *Herald* will be in Harlem, and I'll be in hell!"

In fact, the Herald Building became an architectural showcase, but its location in mid-Manhattan was a traffic nightmare for distributors and its pressrooms a summer inferno for its pressmen.

Now, Bennett's new infatuation was his favorite symbol: the hoot owl. He had run editorials in his New York and Paris editions urging the preservation of the owl species. At his father's estate in Washington Heights overlooking Manhattan and the Hudson River, Bennett again called on Stanford White to erect a 125-foot-tall stone owl standing on a 75-foot-tall pedestal, designed to hold his own future sarcophagus.

Tourists walking the circular staircase inside the owl-shaped tower would see Bennett's empty coffin suspended on two steel chains and pay their respects before reaching the top and enjoying a magnificent view of the city below.

The commodore worked over the plans, saying that the owl must glower "quite ferociously," be made of glazed granite and become a landmark even before he died. It would also overlook General Ulysses S. Grant's tomb on Riverside Drive. Bennett had fiercely opposed Grant when he ran for a second term in the White House.

Stanford White completed his owl plans, and sculptor O'Connor created a clay model of the owl. But when architect White was shot on June 25, 1906, on the roof garden of the original Madison Square Garden Building by the irate playboy husband of White's former girlfriend, Evelyn Nesbit, Bennett decided it was a premonition of bad fortune if he were to build the seventy-five-foot-tall owl. He tore up the plans.

And when the *Herald*'s New York editors wired Bennett, then in Paris, asking how they should treat White's murder story, Bennett replied, "Give him hell!" Apparently, his own long life of bachelor infidelities gave him no feelings of mercy.

Joseph Pulitzer's *New York World* and William Randolph Hearst's *Journal* brought shrieking headlines and gaudy exploits to the press wars in New York more extreme than those in the *Herald*'s heyday. But the sinking of the battleship *Maine* and the Spanish Civil War brought the *New York Herald* back to life. Bennett had hired former navy officers as reporters, and they practiced the reporting of cold hard facts. When Commodore Dewey sailed into Manila Bay, it was the *Herald* correspondent who gave our U.S. president the news.

The short war against Spain brought the *Herald* circulation back to 500,000 copies a day and its profit back to $1 million a year. This brought Bennett back to life. He financed Marconi's wireless telegraph experiments and paid him $5,000 to provide coverage of the America's Cup yacht race in 1899.

The *Herald* launched a campaign against Hearst's bid to be governor of New York State in 1904 and again in 1906. Hearst blamed his losses on Bennett and retaliated by attacking the *Herald*'s sleazy brothel and prostitution advertising. This cut deeply into the *Herald*'s finances. The *Herald* had to pay over $670,000 in fines and much more in lost ad revenue. They were the same sort of ads Hearst was printing in his California newspapers.

A few months later, Hearst announced that he would no longer seek political office, which delighted Bennett. The *Herald* had lambasted the ice-cold treatment W.H. Hearst's newspapers had given to the assassination of President William McKinley by the anarchist Leon Czolgosz on September 6, 1901, and Vice President Teddy Roosevelt's succession as president.

Bennett blamed Hearst for openly promoting the violence in a contemporaneous bonfire incident that killed seventeen people. Hearst fought lawsuits charging him with carelessness in arranging those fireworks protests for twenty years before paying off the fines.

By the summer of 1914, at age seventy-three, Bennett had turned out to be a thrifty Scottish miser. He sold his magnificent ocean yacht to the Russian navy. He had stopped throwing his money around. And his business representatives in New York were sober. The commodore was taking a firm grip on his businesses.

The *New York Herald* circulation peak during the Spanish-American War was 511,000 a day. Now, it was 60,000 and losing hundreds of thousands a year. With the new World War I jitters evoked by Germany's Kaiser Wilhelm on the European continent, it rose to 92,000, and by 1918, it had reached 128,000. That was small potatoes when compared to the *New York Times*, the *World* or the *Tribune and Journal.*

Commodore Bennett had always referred to the Germans as the "Bosh" and despised Kaiser Wilhelm even more than William Randolph Hearst. Even when German troops swept into Belgium in August 1914, Bennett predicted they would be defeated by Christmas. But on September 3, the French government moved to Bordeaux, along with all but one of the French newspapers, the *Paris Temps*, and the *Paris Herald.*

The *Temps* left for Bordeaux when the German troops reached the capital's outer defense ring. Bennett offered his staff and pressmen the option of leaving. A stenographer, two printers and four others in the pressroom, as well as six reporters, stuck with Bennett, who predicted the Germans were overstretched.

The commodore did many of the headlines and editing and even wrote some of the stories. The *Paris Herald* was reduced to a two-page fly sheet, with the second page given over to French translations to keep the remaining residents of the city informed.

On September 10, the Allied headquarters announced that a wedge had been driven between the First and Second German armies, and they were retreating to the Marne and Aisne Rivers. The next day, the *Herald* reported about the heroic role played by the Paris taxicab armies.

September 10 was also the same day that Commodore Bennett was married at the Paris American Church altar to the Baroness de Reuter, formerly Maud Potter of Philadelphia.

A few witnesses were secured for the ceremony, but no announcement was made in any of Bennett's newspapers. Bennett, since breaking his engagement to Caroline May, always boasted, "I suppose no woman who ever lived could get along with me as a wife!"

Maud had married Baron George de Reuter in 1891 and lived with him in Paris until his death in 1909. His family had founded the British Reuter news wire service. She had been friends with Bennett for years, but the marriage was a total surprise to Bennett's friends and employees. She lived in his apartment on the Avenue d'Lena until her own death in 1946.

More surprising still because of his frequent sarcasm about religion, Bennett then joined the Protestant Episcopal Church. How unpredictable was that? Equally unpredictable was the fact that the old Jimmy Bennett was dead or at least tamed.

Cabaret restaurants and café proprietors in Paris suffered a deep financial loss. And when Bennett got large bills from Maud's dressmaker, he raised the sale price of the *Paris Herald*. Bennett also postponed his honeymoon until he could be assured that the *Paris Herald* would keep running.

The new Mrs. Bennett was a longtime friend of Paris's resident American colony. It included such socialites as Mrs. William K. Vanderbilt (known familiarly as Alva); Mr. Herman Harjes, the American representative of J.P. Morgan, and his wife, Frederica Berwind Harjes; James Hazen Hyde, who had fled New York during the investigation of his insurance company; and Harry and Elizabeth Drexel Lehr.

Bennett's *Paris Herald* was continuously predicting the U.S. entry into the defense of Paris, and late in 1916, he traveled across the Atlantic by ship to drum up support in New York and Washington, D.C.

Then, at 6:30 p.m. on June 14, 1917, the ramrod-straight John J. Pershing stepped onto the platform at Paris's Gare du Nord to the cheers of hundreds of Frenchmen, who expected that the American Expeditionary Forces would not be far behind.

But Russia had been broken, and the Bosh were transferring their Eastern forces to their trenches in France. Pershing hired a former New York news reporter to help him handle Bennett, who was demanding that troops be rushed to the French trenches before the American army was trained and the navy ships built to bring them across the Atlantic.

At the June welcoming party for Pershing, Mr. and Mrs. Bennett watched with approval as the general waltzed a handsome widow lady, Louise Brooks, around the ballroom all evening. That lady would later become Mrs. (General) Douglas MacArthur. The Bennetts decided Pershing possessed the right cavalryman's élan.

Because of the *Paris Herald*'s iron support of the Allied cause against the Germans, the Bennetts frequently enjoyed cigars and brandy at Pershing's rented mansion in the Rue de Varennes (a house once owned by a Napoleonic general). However, a Pershing diary entry noted that Bennett was "more aggressive than ever about throwing in the American forces before they were ready to go."

With American forces now arriving by the thousands, the *Paris Herald*'s circulation in early 1918 rose to 100,000 copies daily. Then, in late 1918, Bennett caught a bad cold. To hasten his recovery, with his seventy-seventh birthday approaching on May 10, he and his wife moved to his grand mansion at Beaulieusur Mer on the Riviera.

The commodore was obsessed with his belief that he would die at age seventy-seven, just like his father. Then, during a séance in Monte Carlo, a clairvoyant warned that when his two dogs died, a member of his family would die also.

"She saw my death in her cards," he told Mrs. Bennett, according to her friend, Elizabeth Drexel Lehr.

On the morning of May 10, his seventy-seventh birthday, Bennett suffered a massive brain hemorrhage. Doctors from Paris arrived, but on May 14, at 5:15 a.m., his heart stopped. He had predicted his death within four days.

The *Paris Herald* announced its publisher's death in a very brief obituary, as Bennett would have wished. The *New York Times* obit called him "the founder of the modern newspaper."

Bennett was buried in a little cemetery at Passy, where the French statesman George Clemenceau, known as the tiger, was also buried. Mrs. Bennett arranged for brief funeral services at Paris's Trinity Church. By his own instructions, no name, date of birth or death date was engraved on the stone. But on each corner of the stone was carved the figure of an owl, his favorite symbol.

## RICHARD M. HUNT

### *Lives Modestly, Goes from "Sticks" to "Palaces"*

He built the pedestal and base for Frederic Bartholdi's 1886 Statue of Liberty at the New York City Harbor entrance. He was also the first

American architect to have studied at the prestigious École des Beaux Arts in Paris. By the time Richard Morris Hunt returned in 1855 at the age of twenty-seven to open an office in New York City, he had already served as second in command under Hector Lefuel in the design of a new wing to the Louvre Palace, in Paris, called the Pavilion de la Bibliothèque, opposite the Palais Royal.

Hunt was known in his day as the dean of American architects. He was a founder and served as secretary, and later as president, of the American Institute of Architects. And Hunt established his own atelier for teaching apprentice architects in New York in 1857, when he built the so-called three-story Studio Building at 51 West Tenth Street.

It had some twenty-five studio apartments for artists and designers measuring fifteen by twenty-five to twenty by thirty feet, with high ceilings and excellent lighting, a janitor's office and, at the back of the structure, the two-story exhibition hall with a domed skylight and passageways leading to the studios. What a setup for artists and architects' social parties, as well as a place to entertain clients!

Hunt himself moved in in 1858, along with such artists as John LaFarge, John F. Kensett and Frederick Church. The Studio Building served as a center for artists and "idea men" until it was finally torn down in the late 1950s.

Even before he had moved into his new studio, Hunt had begun to provide architectural instruction to a few pupils, utilizing many elements of Beaux-Arts teaching he had learned in Paris.

Richard Hunt was the fourth of five children of a moderately wealthy Vermont congressman who died when Richard was four; he was fourteen when his mother decided to take the whole family to France for their education because of his older brother William's poor health. William Morris Hunt came under the influence of such French artists as Couture and Millet, later becoming a well-known artist in America, working in French styles.

His brother William was not as keen on the hustle and bustle of New York City life as Richard, and after a short stint in Boston, he decided that Newport, Rhode Island, had much more of the charm of the French countryside. And so had a number of Boston intellectuals and artists such as William Wadsworth Longfellow, Louis Agassiz and George W. Curtis and their families. With a population of about ten thousand permanent residents, Newport was still a quiet place.

In 1856, William bought a little cottage called Hill Top, where the Viking Hotel now stands. Behind it, he built a two-story studio in the rear garden with an artist's painting room on the second floor. And he was soon joined by such artists as John LaFarge and William James.

While Richard was visiting his brother at Hill Top in 1860, he met Catherine Howland of Newport, married her within a year and began work on the J.N.A. Griswold House, a short distance south of the Redwood Library at the corner of Old Beach Road and Bellevue Avenue. After a little renovation, it's now the home of the Newport Art Association's Art Museum.

The elaborate multiple gables, crossbeams, dormers and windows represented a striking design to Newporters and to summer visitors from New York and Boston who had arrived on those multi-decked Fall River line steamships.

Richard once told his son that he must remember, above all, "it's your client's money you're spending. Your business is to get the best results you can, following their wishes. If they want you to build a house upside down, standing on its chimney, it is up to you to do it and still get the best possible result!"

Richard applied his own advice to the clients he worked for building their many mansions on Bellevue and Ochre Point Avenues—such as Chateau Sur Mer, Marble House, Belcourt Castle and the Breakers.

Chateau Sur Mer was built originally for retiring China trade merchant William Shepard Wetmore in 1852. Wetmore died ten years later, leaving this Italianate-style villa to his sixteen-year-old son, George. After studies at Yale and Harvard, in the 1870s, George embarked on a nine-year honeymoon while Richard Hunt transformed the mansion into the Second Empire style of Napoleon III with a Mansard roof.

George served two terms as governor of Rhode Island and three six-year terms as U.S. senator from Rhode Island, but Hunt knew his client had a sense of humor. So the Florentine decorator Luigi Frulini provided carved walnut dining room paneling showing little cherub-like figures drinking wine flanked by witches holding wine pitchers. And the ceiling painting over the table shows George's four-year-old daughter, Edith, dancing with wine-guzzling cherubs, painted by the Italian artist Annibale Gatti.

In addition to his basement wine cellar, George had a second wine cellar in his tower office; it's clear that Richard Hunt played to his client's wishes.

The original Chateau Sur Mer was built in 1852 on Bellevue Avenue. The same year, Newport's great real estate developer Alfred Smith was extending the fifty-foot-wide avenue from Narragansett Avenue all the way to the soon-to-be-exclusive luxurious Spouting Rock Beach Association at Bailey's Beach, "where the Great Ones of the Earth came to play!"

By the winter of 1853–54, sixty new houses were built here, real estate values had tripled and Smith was the seventh-wealthiest man in Newport.

And a year earlier, in 1852, renowned architects Calvert Vaux and Andrew Jackson Downing had built the Italianate-style Beechwood Mansion farther down Bellevue and opposite Rovensky Park for New York dry goods merchant Daniel Parish.

But in 1881, Mrs. William Backhouse Astor Jr. (she shortened the Backhouse to the letter "B" when outhouses were being phased out), bought Beechwood Mansion for $190,000 and called in architect Richard Hunt for a $2 million renovation, including a ballroom that would be able to accommodate up to four hundred guests—just like the one in her New York City mansion.

Just two years later, in 1883, Mrs. William K. Vanderbilt (née Alva Erskin Smith of Mobile, Alabama) broke down the high society barrier Mrs. William B. Astor and Ward McAllister had erected to protect New York high society from the "unworthy" back in 1872.

That's when McAllister, from Savannah, Georgia, arrived in New York City with his plan to appoint some twenty-five so-called patriarchs from old New York families, and each was charged with vetting and selecting four ladies and five gentlemen for invitations to Mrs. Astor's annual Patriarch's Ball. That invitation gave entry to other balls given by other patriarchs, where each invite was observed for "worthiness" in the next round of invitations.

The four Vanderbilt brothers and four sisters were not accepted by Mrs. Astor, possibly because their grandfather, Commodore Cornelius Vanderbilt, was still involved in "trade"—railroads—spit a lot of tobacco and used a lot of "four-letter words."

So in 1882, Alva (Mrs. William K. Vanderbilt), got her husband to hire architect Richard Hunt to build them the greatest Second Empire French chateau New Yorkers had ever seen at 660 Fifth Avenue. On completion, she sent out 1,200 invitations to a Great Costume Ball, but none to Mrs. Astor.

The year 1883 was when Mrs. Astor's daughter was having her debut into society, and she was desperate to attend Alva's fantastic costume ball. Her mother sent her footman with her calling card to Alva's new mansion and voila, the Vanderbilts were in.

Now, Richard Hunt actually got the Vanderbilts into Mrs. Astor's high society. Twelve years later, when Mrs. Astor hired Hunt to build her a new Fifth

Avenue mansion, she told him that her new ballroom must accommodate up to 1,200 guests. She had broadened her standards considerably!

But while Mrs. Astor had hired Hunt to enlarge and add the ballroom at Beechwood for four hundred guests in 1881 at a cost of $2 million, she was completely outspent seven years later. In 1888, Alva's husband, William K. Vanderbilt, hired Hunt to build the Marble House next door to Beechwood at the reputed cost of $11 million—$7 million of that to purchase rare marbles from Numidia and Italy.

William K. reportedly gave Marble House—which Hunt had modeled after the Petit Trianon on the grounds of the Versailles Palace for Madame de Pompadour—to Alva as a thirty-ninth birthday present.

The Gold Room or Grand Salon features a ceiling painting showing Athena, the goddess of wisdom and war, stealing a youth from his love and surrounded by gold-leafed wall panels illustrating nude figures from Greek mythology.

Alva spent time with Richard Hunt in Paris during the four years before Marble House was completed in 1892, and he worked very hard to satisfy her ideas and interests.

Sadly, Alva divorced William K. three years later—after twenty years of marriage and three children—and one year after that she married their mutual friend Oliver Hazard Perry Belmont and moved into Belcourt, also a Hunt-designed mansion just a little farther south on Bellevue Avenue.

When Oliver died in 1908, he left his entire estate to Alva, and she moved back into Marble House and became a pioneer in the women's suffrage movement. And after the Nineteenth Amendment was passed by Congress in 1920 giving women the right to vote, Alva continued to work for women's rights until her death at the age of eighty in 1933.

But back on August 19, 1892, Richard and Catherine Hunt attended the first house-warming party given by Alva and William K. at Marble House. In November 1892, the nearby Breakers mansion, owned by William K's older brother, Cornelius Vanderbilt II, burned to the ground because of a faulty furnace. Then Cornelius called on Richard Hunt to build them a new Breakers.

The Vanderbilts were Hunt's greatest patrons, and when he began work on the Breakers, he was at the height of his career, with major buildings underway in five cities, including the 255-room French Gothic–style Biltmore Mansion for George Washington Vanderbilt in Asheville, North Carolina. The year before, he had completed the great Main Administration Building at the 1893 Columbia Exposition in Chicago.

Cornelius II was married in 1857 to Alice Claypoole Gwenne from Cincinnati, Ohio. They had met while both were teaching Sunday school at St. Bartholomew's Church in New York City, and he had inherited $67 million upon the death of his father, William Henry Vanderbilt, in 1885. William K. got $65 million, and their two younger brothers and four sisters inherited $10 million each. Their father's will was designed to keep the $200 million New York Central Railroad stock in the hands of the two oldest sons.

At Cornelius's suggestion, Hunt's initial design for the new Breakers was in the style of a modest French chateau, but with Alice's sister-in-law at Marble House holding parties even grander than Mrs. Astor's, Hunt remodeled the Breakers after the grand seaside Renaissance palazzi in Genoa, Italy.

The Breakers is built of Indiana limestone and loaded with sculptural detail, with seventy rooms on five levels, the first floor covering some twenty-four thousand square feet or slightly more than half an acre of this thirteen-acre waterfront site.

It is designed as a summer palace, and the loggias, terraces and arcades for outdoor activities were made as an integral part of the design. It had high ceilings, especially in the two-story dining room and great hall, and other large rooms, some flowing into one another. So despite its balanced design, it was given an open and airy character appropriate to summer living. And it embodied Hunt's favorite architectural qualities of "harmony, dignity and repose."

But it also played to Alice Vanderbilt's personal tastes. She had four sons and three daughters. One daughter died of scarlet fever at age five. Her oldest son, William Henry II, died of typhoid fever at Yale University only three months before their original Breakers burned to the ground because of that faulty furnace.

Hunt knew of Alice's grief and her deep love for her sons, as well as her deeply religious feelings, so the rooms are decorated with little winged cherubs, as probably ordered by Hunt via his interior decorators, Jules Allard et Fils in Paris.

How else to explain fifty winged cherubs in the fifty- by fifty-foot-wide and fifty-foot-high Great Entrance Hall? There are four on the double corner archways in each of the room's corners for a total of sixteen. At the top of the four half columns on each side of the room are now faded but originally highly polished bronze cherubs—another sixteen. There are two bronze lamp stands standing on each side of the hall with cherubs on top, as well as ten carved cherub figures and two lions' heads carved on the face of the limestone fireplace.

But that's not all. There are fifty more cherubs on the columns of the music room, ten in the morning room and five in the great spectacular dining hall, which measures forty-two by thirty-eight feet and rises almost fifty feet to a dramatic ceiling painting showing the sun goddess Aurora riding on a chariot and heralding the dawn. The painting is attributed to renowned French artist Paul Baudry, who painted the ceilings of the Paris Opera House.

Also, there are a dozen life-size Olympic-style male athlete statues on either side of the ornate oval ceiling windows and twelve columns of rose alabaster with gilt bronze capitals, as well as two chandeliers and twelve wall sconces of French Baccarat crystal—piped for gas and wired for electricity. In addition, the dining room table can open in all four directions to seat up to thirty-four guests. What a party!

And there are four more winged cherubs in the billiard or pool room, two of these on the glazed tile ceiling, which shows them seated in a Roman bath with their mother, who is looking down at a turtle crawling on the floor. The scene clearly reflects Hunt's strong sense of humor.

Alice is reputed to have complained repeatedly to Hunt about the long time it was taking to finish the massive seventy-room, five-level house—two and a quarter years—while sister-in-law Alva was holding record-setting parties at Marble House. So of course, Hunt had himself portrayed as the turtle, crawling slowly along while she looks down saying, "Hurry up!"

Hunt was truly at the height of his career when he died on July 31, 1895, at age sixty-seven—just three weeks before the first party at the Breakers. That was when Cornelius and Alice held a midnight ball for their oldest daughter, Gertrude, and just a year before she married Harry Payne Whitney in the Breakers' spectacularly ornate Music Room.

On August 28, 1895, William K. and Alva Vanderbilt held a coming-out party for their daughter Consuelo at Marble House. It was attended by the ninth Duke of Marlborough, first cousin to Winston Churchill. Consuelo married the duke on November 6, 1895, and moved into Blenheim Palace in Woodstock, England.

At the front entrance portico to the Breakers, there is a statue of a lady dressed in a suit of armor, wearing a helmet and carrying a sword. She is not Athena, goddess of wisdom and war, as enshrined by Alva at Marble House, but rather Joan of Ark, in keeping with Alice's deeply religious sentiments, known so well by architect Richard Morris Hunt.

Richard Morris Hunt was buried in Newport's Island Cemetery on Farewell Street, where you can also find the graves of George Peabody Wetmore and Newport real estate developer Alfred Smith, his wife and their daughter.

## Stanford White

### *"Voluptuary and Pervert—Dies the Death of a Dog!" Said* Vanity Fair *in 1906*

In 1853, Newport real estate developer Alfred Smith completed the fifty-foot-wide Bellevue Avenue, and sixty new houses were built here. This was also the year that the New York City Council approved the creation of Central Park and the Crystal Palace Exposition opened in New York's Bryant Park behind what is now the New York Public Library at Forty-second Street and Fifth Avenue.

And coincidentally, architect Stanford White was born on November 9, 1853, on East Tenth Street, near St. Mark's Church on Bowery, where there were fifty-two taverns and twenty-seven oyster houses. Could that possibly explain why "Holy Moses, gin and seltzer!" was Stanford White's favorite expression? Also, coincidentally, 1853 was the year the New York Central Railroad was established from a union of twelve small lines.

White's father, Richard Grant White, had a six-hundred-volume library of Shakespeare's poetry. He worked as a reporter for the *New York Courier* and *Enquirer* and alternately for the New York Customhouse because his too strongly expressed views about political corruption in New York kept making him change jobs.

"Stanny" was the youngest of Richard White's two sons and at age sixteen had a strong talent and desire to be an artist. But two of his father's close friends, John LaFarge and Frederick Law Olmsted, recommended architecture as more remunerative.

Olmsted took Stanny to the New York office of Henry Hobson Richardson, the second American architect to have studied at the École des Beaux Arts in Paris (after Richard Hunt). Richardson hired Stanny on the spot. And Richardson's office manager was Charles McKim, the third American architect to have studied at the École and an excellent teacher for young quick-learning Stanny.

Richardson was jolly, liked to drink with his staff and clients and, like Richard Hunt, said, "I'll plan anything a man wants, from a cathedral to a chicken coop. That's the way I make my living!"

Richardson's technique was to provide a rough sketch of a project to his draftsmen and make numerous suggestions as the project developed so in the end the final design was his own. But his staff had learned to "think for themselves."

The first house to which White contributed work in Richardson's office was a large summer cottage overlooking the water in Middletown, Rhode Island, for Frank Williams Andrews in 1872 and 1873. It was inspired by English architect Richard Norman Shaw's first Queen Anne–style house built in 1868 in England, with multiple gables and small-paned windows, but here a variety of shingle patterns was added to further break up the wall spaces.

Also in 1872, Richardson's office won the commission to build Boston's Trinity Church, and McKim's designs were turned over to eighteen-year-old Stanny when McKim resigned to set up his own office in New York. Then White redesigned the church tower.

White also contributed to Richardson's design of wealthy banker William Watts Sherman's Queen Anne–style mansion on Newport's Shepard Avenue, opposite Chateau Sur Mer, between 1874 and 1876.

Sherman had married George Wetmore's sister, Annie Derby Wetmore, and years later Sherman called on White to build the New York Metropolitan Club.

In February 1878, having completed numerous projects in New England and New York with Richardson's staff over eight years and having saved enough funds for a fourteen-month study tour of Europe, Stanny's resignation was accepted with deep regret.

Stanny moved into the Paris studio apartment of a former New York friend, the sculptor Augustus Saint-Gaudens, and traveled widely in France and Italy, as well as enjoying some of the Bohemian lifestyle.

In September 1879, at the age of twenty-five, Stanny joined the New York architectural firm of McKim and Mead on the top floor of 57 Broadway, and his first major project was the interior decorative detail and elaborate courtyard trelliswork of the Newport Casino.

This commission came from James Gordon Bennett Jr., a great and colorful sportsman and commodore of the New York Yacht Club, who had inherited $7 million and taken over as owner and publisher of the *New York Herald* newspaper after his father's death in 1872.

The Newport Casino was also to be in the Shingle style with multiple gables, small-paned windows, multiple piazzas or porches, reading and dining rooms, card and billiard rooms and clubrooms and bachelors' quarters. It would very soon come to serve as a pattern for similar clubs across the country.

That Shingle style had been inspired by a summer tour of New England colonial buildings explored by the future architectural partners two years earlier. So the Casino cemented an important business relationship with Bennett and opened the door to McKim, Mead and White's firm for a long series of commissions for mansions, public buildings and (especially for White) clubhouses.

Among the best known of these by White are Madison Square Garden (seating seventeen thousand), the Metropolitan Club, the Century Association Club, the Colony Club and the Players' Club—all in New York, and all but the first still around.

The best-known works by McKim were the Boston Public Library, the now-leveled New York Pennsylvania Railway Station, the Narragansett Pier Casino (on the mainland and across the bay from Newport and Jamestown Island) and the Lowe Library and other buildings at Columbia University, in New York.

But what about the third partner, William Rutherford Mead, whom they affectionately used to call "the dummy"? He was the one who managed the payroll, hired and fired and supervised the financial arrangements, as well as planned construction engineering, heating and plumbing and kept the architectural projects moving. He was a graduate of Amherst College, a student of the Academia de Belle Arti in Florence, Italy, and smoked a lot of cigars.

McKim, Mead and White came to be known as the most successful architectural firm in the country. By 1910, it had a staff of ninety-two and had handled more than seven hundred commissions with total construction costs of more than $36 million.

Upon completion of the Newport Casino in 1881, its dance hall and theater, band concerts, tennis matches and horse shows became the early center for Newport's Gilded Age society, and the Queen Anne Shingle style immediately brought McKim, Mead and White commissions for five other mansions here with variations in that same style.

The largest of the five is Ochre Point, built by the firm between 1879 and 1881 on Ochre Point Avenue, between Narragansett Avenue and Webster Street, overlooking the water but surrounded by high hedges for privacy. In the Shingle style, it has multiple gables, cross-gables, wide piazzas and small-paned windows.

It was built for Robert Goelet, who, with his brother Ogden Goelet, owned large blocks of New York real estate lying between Union Square at Fourteenth Street and northward to Forty-seventh Street with an estimated 1870 book value of approximately $100 million.

Among other Shingle-style summer homes built by the firm in the period was the Isaac Bell Jr. house on Bellevue at the corner of Perry Street, built for James Gordon Bennett Jr.'s younger sister, Jeannette. She married Bell, a major investor in the transatlantic cable company used by her brother's newspapers in New York and Paris.

In decorating Jeannette's bedroom of her new house, Stanny used the same meticulous colored basket–weave ceiling decoration he had employed in the ballroom ceiling in Bennett's Newport Casino. She must have liked it!

From 1881 to '83, McKim and White were building variations of those Shingle-style houses for Samuel Coleman on Red Cross Avenue and for Samuel Tilton on Sunnyside Place.

In 1881, White designed the pedestal and base for his friend sculptor Augustus Saint-Gaudens's monument to Admiral David G. Farragut in New York's Madison Square Park.

Almost ten years later, in 1890, Stanny completed his most dramatic work: the magnificent Madison Square Garden Amphitheater seating seventeen thousand spectators, with a roof garden, theater and concert hall, as well as a 341-foot-tall tower with an elevator. There were also seven stories of two-room apartments in that tower, one of which Stanny rented himself.

On the tower's pinnacle, Stanny's friend Saint-Gaudens created an eighteen-foot-tall sheet copper statue of the Greek hunting goddess Diana, very scantily clothed. Saint-Gaudens later had to replace it with a svelte thirteen-foot model of the goddess of the hunt.

And 1890 was also the year that Stanny's Washington Memorial Arch on Washington Square in Greenwich Village was dedicated by the newly elected Republican mayor, William Strong—to the chagrin of Tammany Hall Democrats. A very busy year for Stanny, as usual.

In 1891, Tessie Oelrich and her younger unmarried sister, Virginia Fair, bought the original Rosecliff Mansion on Newport's famed Bellevue Avenue, just two doors north of Alva Vanderbilt's newly built $11 million Marble House.

After settling lawsuits over the inheritance of their late father, James Fair's silver fortune in Virginia City, Nevada, in 1898, Tessie and Virginia hired

Stanny to build them a brand-new $2.5 million Rosecliff, modeled after the Grand Trianon, which was built in 1690 as a garden retreat for Louis XIV by Jules Hardouin Mansart.

The H-shaped mansion, with its great French-style arched windows interspersed with Ionic half columns or pilasters, is made of white-glazed terra cotta (to look like marble).

Between the wings of the H is the eighty- by forty-foot Rococo-style ballroom with its ocean-view terrace on one side and a formal French-style parterre garden terrace on the other—all surrounded by extensive lawn vistas.

Symmetry with variation is everywhere, like in the entry hall on one side of the H. Inside are four arches, one on each side: one for the grand staircase, one for the reception room, one for the ballroom and one coming in.

And the forty- by eighty-foot ballroom has three arches on the short sides, going to the billiard and dining rooms, and five on the long sides, all with doors going to the water-view terrace on the east side and to the garden-view terrace on the west.

Moreover, the ballroom ceiling is interspersed with painted flowerpots and images of classical ladies—too intricate for clear description but reflecting Stanny's theme of symmetry and variation.

After four years, in 1902, White completed Rosecliff, but it might have been done sooner had Tessie not insisted on giving parties by covering unfinished areas with masses of flowers—probably at Stanny's suggestion because he liked to give parties with his clients.

In 1900, a new musical called *Floridora* opened in the New York Casino on Broadway and Thirty-ninth Street, and there Evelyn Nesbit, playing a bit part as a Spanish dancer, was spotted by Stanford White, who, in addition to being a great designer and party planner, had a reputation for secret liaisons with young actresses.

White persuaded the mother of sixteen-year-old Evelyn to allow her daughter to attend a luncheon at his Twenty-fourth Street hideaway apartment with three others. That luncheon grew into a five-year secret romance until, in 1905, Evelyn married the mentally erratic wealthy playboy Harry Thaw from Pittsburgh.

After Evelyn returned from Europe with her husband in 1906, Stanford stupidly confided in a mutual friend that he intended to win back Evelyn's affections, and to feed Harry's jealous temperament, Evelyn passed on this remark to her husband, not realizing the radical reaction it would trigger.

Stanny, after dining with his two sons in a nearby restaurant, took the elevator in the Madison Square Garden tower's roof garden theater to hear the performance of the musical *Mamzelle Champagne*, which he had had helped to finance. White took a table near the stage, where the tenor Harry Short was singing the song "I Could Love a Thousand Girls!"

Thaw, who had been sitting at a rear table with Evelyn, pulled a pistol out of his coat pocket, walked up to White's table and shot him three times in the head, shouting, "You'll never go out with that woman again!" He threw the gun on the floor. The music stopped, and the audience dashed for the exits. The police arrived and took Thaw into custody.

An autopsy later indicated that the fifty-two-year-old White probably would have died within a year of Bright's disease and liver failure. But the subsequent two long trials of Harry Thaw on a charge of murder were perhaps the most sensational in twentieth-century journalism.

The first three-month trial ended with a hung jury; the second was over in three weeks with the verdict "innocent on grounds of insanity." After two terms in an insane asylum, Thaw was released in 1925 and died of a heart attack in 1947 at the age of seventy-six in Miami Beach.

Evelyn died in 1967 at the age of eighty-two in a California nursing home, where she taught ceramics and sculpture following a checkered career as a dancer; running speakeasies in New York, Atlantic City and New Orleans; writing two autobiographies; and earning $50,000 as a consultant on the 1955 movie *The Girl in the Red Velvet Swing*, with Ray Milland as White, Joan Collins as Evelyn and Farley Granger as Thaw.

In her first autobiography she lamented her effort during Harry's trial to save a man she didn't really love from being punished for killing the man she really loved. But she had known all along that Stanny never would have left his wife and children for her.

Stanford White was vilified by the press in 1906 as a seducer and corruptor of young girls. Many of his old friends distanced themselves from him, including *New York Herald* owner James Gordon Bennett, for whom Stanny had built the Herald Building on Herald Square in 1893.

But when the *Herald* editors asked Bennett how to handle the White murder story, he wired back from Paris in traditional journalese: "Give him hell!"

White's last architectural work, now gone but which some critics called his greatest, was the new Madison Square Presbyterian Church, just across the street from the old one. Its rector, the Reverend Dr. Charles Park, famous for his denunciation of New York's Tammany Hall bosses, praised White's work in building the new church and lamented his death at the church dedication ceremonies.

Three years later, in 1909, Stanford's beloved and faithful partner, Charles McKim, long in poor health, died at age sixty-two. His friend August Saint-Gaudens died of cancer in 1907. But the dependable third partner, "the dummy" William Mead, carried on the work of the firm with new partners until his retirement in 1920. He died in 1928.

*III*

# COACHMAN'S DRIVE-AROUND TOUR

## Downtown Harbor Front and Colonial Newport

### *Navy's First Headquarters in Newport*

In addition to leading the thirteen colonies into gaining independence, Newport had become the headquarters of the U.S. Navy and continued this role until 1953, when the headquarters were moved to Norfolk and Newport News, Virginia.

Newport's wharves and facilities had been devastated by the British occupying forces. Some merchants returned. Efforts to revive trade were struck another blow in the War of 1812 and yet another by a great storm in 1815. The port never regained its prowess in shipping. Its revival as a resort for tourists came in the 1840s with the inauguration of the Fall River line steamships, which provided daily service to New York for ninety years, until 1937.

### *J.P. Jones Christens the First Navy Ship*

It was the navy that kept Newport's economy afloat. John Paul Jones commissioned the first U.S. Navy ship, the *Katy*, as the *Providence* on this island. And the first naval battle of the Revolutionary War took place just north of the Newport Bridge.

Newport Bridge was renamed after Rhode Island's recently retired U.S. senator Claiborne Pell. The bridge was opened in 1969 with a span of 2.5 miles, making it the longest suspension bridge in New England. The span is two hundred feet above the water to accommodate huge U.S. Navy aircraft carriers, which are no longer based here.

## *Where the First Colonists Kept Goats*

Goat Island got its name when the first colonists kept their goats on it instead of building fences. The stone marks the site of Fort George, from which the colonists fired thirteen cannon rounds at the gunboat HMS *St. George*.

In 1869, this island was designated a navy torpedo manufacturing station; two years later, the first propelled torpedo was built here. In 1880, the first boat specifically designed to fire torpedoes was built here. During World War II, seventeen thousand torpedoes were manufactured on this island in huge plants employing twelve thousand in three round-the-clock shifts. In place of those plants, you now see condominiums and the unusually shaped Hyatt Regency Hotel, designed to withstand hurricane-force winds. And across the water to the south is Fort Adams, the first part of it built in 1799 and named after our second president.

## *Navy's Highest Institute of Learning*

Just north of Newport Bridge is Coasters Island, the Navy War College—the U.S. Navy's highest institute of learning. Candidates were required to have 9.5 years of service as officers just to enroll. It was founded in 1884 by Admiral Stephen B. Luce, who also founded the Navy Training Center here the previous year.

The white building with the little cupola was built much earlier, in 1820, as an insane asylum, as well as a pesthouse and workhouse for the poor. Officers studying nuclear strategy in there during the Cold War must have felt quite at home.

In 1951, the Navy Officers' Candidate School was founded on that island, and during its forty-two years in Newport, it graduated 100,573 officers—more than the U.S. Navy Academy at Annapolis, which was also located in Newport during the four years of the American Civil War.

In 1946, Newport was homeport for one hundred of the navy's ships; by 1973, it was down to forty-three ships, and in 1993, the last navy ship left Newport. But many training schools and facilities are still here, and for some years, there were a couple of old aircraft carriers in mothballs.

## *A Museum of Ship Models and Accounts of Navy Battles*

The Navy War College has a museum of ship models and personal accounts of major navy battles that is open to the public.

The group of houses to the north of this causeway to Newport Bridge, and from the seawall back to the railway tracks, is called The Point. Easton's Point was named after the Quaker descendants of Nicholas Easton, who developed it into building lots. More than one hundred of the three hundred or so pre–Revolutionary War houses surviving in Newport today are located there.

The house on the far right was built in 1749. After the Revolution, wealthy privateer Simon Potter (yes, he had a license to plunder French and Spanish ships) gave it to the proprietors of Long Wharf so they could open the first "free" school here for poor children.

Long Wharf is the street running along the water at the far right. It was lined with wharves and sheds, and the wealthy merchants who owned them banded together as early as 1880 to promote Newport trade. They set prices and quality standards in candle making and built the Brick Market (an open market house and grain storage) in the center of town.

## *Where Thirty-one Pirates Were Hanged*

Long Wharf was where the first colonists Easton and Brenton built their first wharves just after settling here in 1639 and where thirty-one pirates were hanged in 1723. The west end of Long Wharf is now owned by the State of Rhode Island and is used by our local lobstermen to keep their boats and bring in their catches. To the north is the Newport Shipyard, Newport's last remaining shipyard.

The second house to the left of the Potter House was owned by Isaac Dayton, who after the Revolution moved to Ohio and helped found the city of Dayton, which still bears his name.

The Isaac Dayton House.

To the left of that house, the two houses before the corner are the home and counting house of the merchant trading family of Jehleel Brenton. Yes, they kept their accounts in the counting house, not just counting their money there.

## *An Outspoken Tory Had to Flee*

One of the finest examples of Colonial houses in America is the Hunter House, first on the waterside of Washington Street (which was originally called Water Street). The south end of this house was built in 1748 by Jonathan Nichols Jr.; the north end was added in 1756 by Joseph Wanton Jr. They were both wealthy merchants, and both served as deputy governors of Rhode Island. But Wanton was an outspoken Tory and had to flee to New York with the British troops when they pulled out in 1779.

The French Admiral de Ternay chose this house for his billet but became ill and died here. He was buried in the Trinity Church cemetery. This house is open to the public through the Preservation Society of Newport County, the largest of several nonprofit educational organizations offering for-fee tours of historic properties in Newport.

The Hunter House contains a fine collection of antique Chippendale-style furniture, hand crafted, in part, by three generations of the Townsend and Goddard cabinetmaking families here in Newport. The collection is probably even more valuable than the finely paneled house.

The Hunter House and garden.

## *Captain William Kidd Buried Treasure?*

Among Newport's better-known pirates were William Mayes Jr., whose father built the Whitehorse Tavern, and Captain Thomas Payne, who retired from pirating and built his retirement home in Jamestown, where the notorious pirate captain William Kidd visited him. That started the rumor that Kidd buried some of his famous treasure there—they say some still dig for it to this day.

America's Cup Avenue was named after the famous sailing race trophy, usually awarded every four years. It is promoted by the New York Yacht Club, which first won the cup off the Isle of Wight in England in 1851 and defended it successfully until Dennis Connor's loss to *Australia II* in 1983.

On the far side of the street is Cardines Baseball Field, built in 1908—four years before Fenway Park in Boston. This is where Babe Ruth, the "Sultan of Swat," began his career in the minor leagues with a team called the Providence Braves. The stadium itself was built by the Works Progress Administration (WPA) in 1937. The field was named after Barnardo Cardines, Newport's first casualty in World War I.

Across the street to the west is the Newport County Convention and Visitors' Information Center, and to its south the Newport Marriott Hotel and the remnant of Long Wharf, where Brenton and Easton built their first wharves in about 1641.

The Visitors' Information Center.

Heading south on America's Cup Avenue, a group of fifty stores on the left were built during a 1975 redevelopment program around the original colonial Brick Market, completed by the Long Warf Merchants Association in 1772.

On the right is the Providence ferry stop and another hotel. A little more to the south are Bannisters and Bowens Wharves. There, in place of the original docks and sheds of the merchants—and a dozen rum distilleries—as well as shipbuilders and sail and rope makers, you will now find restaurants, nightclubs, galleries and condominiums.

## *There Were Twenty-two Rum Distilleries Here*

The Newport Historical Society has reported that in 1770 there were twenty-two rum distilleries here. No wonder Newport was the first vacation resort in America!

The white church spire on the left belongs to Trinity Church, rebuilt in 1726 by Newport's first renowned carpenter-builder (as they were called

Trinity Church, built in 1725.

then), Richard Maunday. The green park around it was dedicated by Queen Elizabeth II herself during her 1976 American bicentennial visit. She named it Queen Anne Square.

The name Queen Anne was chosen because England's Queen Anne began her reign in 1702, the same year that the original Trinity Church was built on this site.

America's Cup Avenue runs into Thames Street, the first street built in Newport. The colonists called it "Tems" Street until after the Revolution, when they started discarding all things English—even their pronunciation of words.

## *Benjamin Franklin Opened the First Post Office on This Site*

Following the divided street as it goes up the hill to the left, the corner post office is on the site of the very first U.S. Post Office. Benjamin Franklin, who in 1753 became the first postmaster for all of the colonies, would visit his older brother James Franklin here. James had earlier taught Benjamin the printing trade when they were living in Boston. After Benjamin ran off to Philadelphia, James moved to Newport and set up a print shop.

In 1732, James published the first newspaper in Newport: the *Rhode Island Gazette*. It was short-lived. But James's wife and son later set up a weekly newspaper, the *Newport Mercury*, in 1758, and it is still being published today as the *Newport Daily News*.

The only divided street in Newport changes its name going up the hill to Memorial Boulevard. The large Gothic-style brownstone church on the right is St. Mary's, the oldest Roman Catholic church in Rhode Island. Built in 1852, it was constructed by the oldest Rhode Island Catholic parish, founded in 1828. And it was in there, on September 12, 1953, that the late Jacqueline Bouvier married then senator John F. Kennedy, our late president.

Spring Street was named after the natural spring once located at its north end and is claimed to be the first paved street in the United States.

The next street is Franklin Street, named after James Franklin, who opened his first print shop here on Washington Square in 1725. The Newport Congregational Church on the right was built of brownstone in 1857, and later the American artist John LaFarge designed the beautiful stained-glass windows for it.

St. Mary's, where JFK married Jacqueline Bouvier.

## *First Street Lit by Gaslight*

Pelham Street is said to be the first street to be lit by gaslight in the United States in the year 1803. The house on the far upper right corner of Pelham belonged to the Italian seascape painter Michael Feleche Corne.

It is said that Corne introduced the tomato to Rhode Island, convincing his neighbors they were good to eat. Previously, they thought tomatoes were poisonous.

You may also notice some examples here of Colonial full third and half houses. People couldn't always afford to build a full house at once, but as families got larger, so did the incentive to add to the houses. The signs on many of these houses bearing the initials "NRF" were placed there by Doris Duke, the tobacco heiress, who died in October 1993, leaving an estate of $1.2 billion. She founded the Newport Restoration Foundation, which has restored some eighty-five colonial period houses in Newport and leases them out to residents under preservation restrictions.

Colony House, built in 1739.

On the left is Trinity Church, then part of the Church of England, known in America as the Episcopal Church. It was built by Newport's first renowned architect, Richard Maunday, in 1725. Now, it's a National Historic Landmark. It is in the style of Christopher Wren, who built so many churches in London after the Great Fire of 1666. George Washington worshiped twice inside, and his pew is now marked with a plaque. Among the colonial era gravestones on the far side is one for Admiral de Ternay, who died at Hunter House and was buried here in ground specially consecrated in this cemetery by his own Roman Catholic chaplain.

The brick building on the left was still operated until recently by Wards Printers, which had operated in this building since its establishment here in 1849.

The second building on the left, Colony House, was built in 1739, again by Richard Maunday, the architect for Trinity Church. From the balcony on the front, Rhode Island declared its independence from Britain on May 4, 1776—two whole months before the other English colonies declared theirs. Rhode Island was the first colony to declare independence but the last to ratify the U.S. Constitution (in 1790 by just two votes).

## *Rhode Island Was Afraid of the Debts of Other States*

Having previously been one of the wealthiest colonies, Rhode Islanders were afraid, among other things, of being stuck with the debts of some of the poorer colonies. No need to worry—they ended up with plenty of their own debts.

The Colony House was the state capitol before the Revolution. General Washington was entertained inside, and the first public Roman Catholic Mass in New England was celebrated here on the death of French Admiral de Ternay.

The square is now called Washington Square. The park in the center is called Eisenhower Park after the Republican president who used to summer here. The streets on either side were originally called Queen Street and Anne Street, but it was never called Queen Anne Square. Originally, it was called The Parade.

The white house at the bottom of the square at the right was built in the early 1700s and enlarged in 1758 by the wealthy merchant Abraham Rodrigues Riviera. In 1803, it was opened as the Savings Bank of Newport. It was the third-oldest bank in the United States until in 1993, when it was taken over by Citizens Bank.

Washington Square with the statue of Oliver Hazard Perry.

This bronze engraving shows Oliver Hazard Perry's brother, Matthew Perry, in 1854 negotiations in Japan that opened that country to Western trade. The engraving is on the base of Matthew's statue in Newport's Touro Park (see his bio on pages 21–23).

The Peter Buloid House.

The Brick Market.

The statue in the center of Eisenhower Park honors Perry, the navy hero who, in 1912, won the surrender of the British fleet on Lake Erie and sent back the cryptic message: "We have met the enemy and they are ours!"

Perry was a Rhode Island native born in Kingston and the brother of Matthew Perry, who is credited with opening Japan to Western trade.

The house behind the statue to the south was built by Peter Buloid in 1755. It was opened in 1794 as the Rhode Island Bank, the first bank in Rhode Island. But in 1818, it was bought for use as a home by Oliver Perry, who died only a year later. The exterior wood sheathing has been cut and painted to look like stone blocks, a procedure common in colonial times that architects called "rustication."

The brick building at the bottom of the square is the Brick Market, built in 1772 to resemble Summerset House in London by Newport's other early renowned architect, Peter Harrison. Harrison constructed two other famous buildings here. This Brick Market was built as an open market house by the proprietors of Long Wharf. It has since served at various times as a city hall, a theater and an art gallery.

## *Newport Historical Society Opened as Modern Museum*

More recently, the Brick Market was further restored by the Newport Historical Society (NHS) and opened as a modern historical museum with video and audio tapes and displays illustrating Newport history from its founding in 1639 through the Gilded Age period and to the present.

Among its jewels is the printing press James Franklin brought from England. He used it to teach his brother Benjamin the trade, and on it he printed his newspapers both here and earlier in Boston. The same press was later owned by Solomon Southwick, who buried it during the British occupation. A Tory neighbor betrayed its location to the British, who dug up the press and printed their own newspaper here.

The brick courthouse to the right of Colony House is where Claus Van Bulow was twice found guilty of attempting to murder his wife, Sunny, by insulin injection. These convictions were set aside on appeal. Claus was retried in a Providence courthouse, where Harvard professor Alan Dershowitz led his defense and won him an acquittal on both counts.

Turning right on Clark Street, the stone building on the right is the Newport Artillery Company Museum, built in 1835 by the Scottish stonemason Alexander McGregor, who built major additions to Fort Adams.

### *King George II Chartered the Newport Artillery Company in 1741*

The Newport Artillery Company's original charter has never been interrupted, making it the oldest standing militia in the country. The house at 14 Clark Street was the home of its pastor and historian, Ezra Styles, who, during the Revolution, became the seventh president of Yale College in New Haven, Connecticut.

### *General de Rochambeau Entertained General Washington Here*

Vernon House was used during the French occupation as the headquarters of General de Rochambeau. He also entertained General Washington there (yes, General Washington slept there, too). That house was built in the early 1700s and was enlarged and "rusticated" by Metcalf Bowler, who lent it to de Rochambeau. But in the 1920s, it was discovered that Bowler was actually a spy, giving rebel secrets to the British.

### *Touro, the Oldest Synagogue in the United States*

Touro Synagogue is the oldest synagogue in the United States. It was built by the architect Peter Harrison, who also built the Brick Market. It was

Touro Synagogue.

dedicated in 1763 by a congregation of eighty Jewish families who had been worshiping in private homes since the first families arrived here in 1658. But the oldest Jewish congregation is in Brooklyn, New York. This is the second-oldest congregation. The building is on an angle to the street so that the ark within would face Jerusalem.

At the end of the street is the Jewish cemetery, where the carved torches on the gates face down to indicate that the lights of the dead have been extinguished.

## BELLEVUE AVENUE—NORTH

At the top of this hill is the beginning of Bellevue Avenue and to the right, the Viking Hotel. (For details on the real estate development of this area, see the biography of Alfred Smith.)

The Viking is the oldest surviving hotel here. It was built in 1926 from funds raised by one hundred of the wealthiest summer residents. Some of

Newport Reading Room, a men's-only club since 1852.

the larger suites of rooms include additional bedrooms for members of the guests' personal staff, including valets and maids.

The building with the wooden fence painted to look like iron is the Newport Reading Room, founded as a men's-only club in 1852 by a group of gentlemen headed by William Shepard Wetmore, who completed his own mansion, Chateau Sur Mer, in the same year. However, the club building was originally constructed about 1835 as a summer hotel.

One of the later members of this exclusive club was James Gordon Bennett Jr., owner of the *New York Herald*—later the *Herald Tribune*—who dared fellow polo player Captain Candy to ride his horse right in through the club's front door.

## *Rode Horse through Club's Front Door*

The Reading Room club members were not amused. Candy was stripped of his temporary membership, and Bennett was severely reprimanded for egging Candy on. This made Bennett so furious that he vowed to build his own club, the Newport Casino.

On the left is the Redwood Library, the original front part built in 1750 by Peter Harrison, who built Touro Synagogue and the Brick Market. It is constructed of "rusticated" wood to look like stone, and it's the oldest

The Redwood Library.

The Griswold House.

library in the country still lending books from the original building. (But it's the seventh-oldest library building.) Its first librarian was the pastor Ezra Styles, later president of Yale. The library founders were all members of the Philosophical Club, and one of them, Abraham Redwood, gave the then considerable sum of £500 to buy the first books, most of which are still among the library's many collections.

## *The First Building by Architect Hunt in Newport*

Next on the left is the Griswold House, built in 1862 in the Stick style for China trade merchant John N.A. Griswold by the famous architect Richard Morris Hunt. Hunt was the first American architect to study at the renowned Paris School of Fine Arts, and this is the first of a half dozen mansions Hunt built in Newport. The best known, of course, are Marble House and the Breakers, built for two Vanderbilt brothers. The Griswold House is now the Newport Art Association's museum. Opposite the museum is Touro Park, donated to Newport by the wealthy merchant Judo Touro.

The Stone Mill.

The Old Stone Mill in the park was immortalized in a poem by Henry Wadsworth Longfellow, who also wrote poems about the Channing Memorial Unitarian Chapel and the Touro Jewish Cemetery.

The Stone Mill may have been built by Rhode Island governor Benedict Arnold, great-great-grandfather of the Revolutionary War traitor who used the stone tower as a windmill about 1658.

## *Tower Built by Twelfth-Century Vikings?*

Some archaeologists cling to the Newport tradition that the tower was actually built by the Vikings in the twelfth century as a celestial observatory. The experts don't agree with one another.

The statue in the center of the green is of Commodore Matthew Calbraith Perry, a Newport native and brother of Oliver Hazard Perry, the hero of the Battle of Lake Erie. Matthew sailed his black-painted ships to Japan in 1853 and again in 1854 and got the first treaty allowing American ships to visit the Japanese port of Shimoda.

## *Sumo Wrestlers at Black Ships Festival*

Today, Perry is credited with opening Japan to the West. And the people of Shimoda, Newport's sister city in Japan, come here each July to host the Black Ships Festival. It features Japanese kite flying, food and sumo wrestlers, all in memory of Perry's black-painted ships visiting Japan in 1854.

Elks Lodge.

Travers Block.

On the right corner is the Elks Lodge, originally built in the Queen Anne style for Countess O'Leary in 1881. This was previously the site of the large Greek Revival–style Atlantic House hotel, built in 1844 for the new flood of southern tourists.

During the Civil War, from 1861 to 1865, the U.S. Navy took over the Atlantic House to use as its naval academy because Annapolis was too close to the Confederacy.

Crossing Memorial Boulevard, the English Tudor beamed building on the left corner is the Travers Block, built in 1875, also by Richard Morris Hunt. There were shops and, on the second floor, bachelor apartments, which were in short supply at the time.

## *Casino Became Center of Newport Social Life*

Next on the left is the innovative family membership clubhouse, the Newport Casino. It was built in 1879–81 for James Gordon Bennett Jr., the *New York Herald* newspaper publisher who got in a pique after being censured when Captain Candy rode his horse into the entrance of the Newport Reading Room.

The Newport Casino quickly became the center of Newport social life, with its horse and flower shows, theater, restaurant, concerts, dances (then called "hops"), card and billiard rooms and twelve grass tennis courts.

Newport Casino.

The casino, which now houses the International Tennis Hall of Fame Museum on the second floor, was the site of the first national tennis championships in 1881, and all other national tennis matches were held here until 1915, when they were moved to Forrest Hills and later to Ocean Meadows.

The grass courts inside are the only ones in the United States still hosting major tennis tournaments each year. The magnificent building, designed by Charles McKim and Stanford White of McKim, Mead and White, not only launched the use of the Shingle style in Newport but also became a model for similar clubhouses across the United States.

## *Kingscote, Short for King's Cottage*

The blue-gray American Gothic Revival–style house beyond the shopping center on the right was built in 1841 by the English architect Richard Upjohn for George Nobel Jones, the largest plantation owner in Savannah, Georgia. Near the end of the Civil War, Jones sold the house to William

Kingscote.

Berkley Villa.

King, another of the China trade merchants who retired to Newport after making their fortunes.

King commissioned the architect Stanford White, who had just finished building the Newport Casino, to build a dining room addition in White's own imitable style. King named the new house Kingscote—short for Kings Cottage—and filled it with Chinese and American antiques. It, too, is open to the public for tours.

Across Bellevue on the left is Berkeley Villa, built in 1910 by the Boston decorator/architect Ogden Codman Jr. in the Colonial Revival style for his cousin Martha Codman, who later married the thirty-years-younger Russian opera singer Maxim Karolik. The singer boasted upon arriving in this country that he had previously heard of only three U.S. cities: New York; Washington, D.C.; and Newport.

## *One of Five Shingle-Style Mansions*

Next is the house built for the wealthy retired cotton futures trader Isaac Bell after his marriage to James Gordon Bennett Jr.'s sister, Jeanette. It is one of the five Shingle-style houses that Stanford White and Charles McKim built here between 1881 and 1883 following the firm's successful completion of the Newport Casino.

Isaac Bell.

The Elms.

The next major mansion on the right is called The Elms, built for the Pennsylvania coal magnate Edward Julius Berwind. Horace Trumbauer, who built the Philadelphia Art Museum, modeled this one after an 1751 French chateau. It cost only $1.4 million, including walls and furnishings—what a buy! Could Mr. Berwind have been bartering coal for limestone?

## *Berwind's Face on Big Urns?*

On the big urns atop the walls, you can see Mr. Berwind's face—clearly a modest man! The house, built in 1899–91, is open to the public, along with its extensive gardens and fountains.

As we turn left on Narragansett Avenue, the house on the southwest corner is now the new headquarters building of the Preservation Society of Newport County, the second and youngest, but with little doubt the wealthiest, of three historical societies here. Since its founding in 1945 to

The Preservation Society of Newport County.

save a merchant's home on the harbor, it has acquired five small and five large historic mansions, two of the latter owned by Vanderbilts.

The Newport Historical Society, founded in 1853, has the Brick Market Museum on Washington Square; a headquarters building and historical library next to Touro Synagogue on Touro Street; the Walton Lyman Hazard House, built in 1675, on lower Broadway and only one block from the Colony House; and the Quaker Meeting House, built in part in 1699, across from the Whitehorse Tavern on Farewell Street (that street just happens to pass through the cemetery as you leave Newport—some coincidence!).

The Newport Restoration Foundation was founded by an American Tobacco Company heiress who saved eighty-five colonial-era houses from destruction and whose father bought Frederick William Vanderbilt's mansion, Rough Point (now open to the public).

## *Senator Pell's Boyhood Home*

The Preservation Society headquarters were actually the boyhood home of Rhode Island's recent senator Clayborn Pell, but the structure was built in the Romanesque Revival style in 1887 for William Osgood, who was married to Commodore Vanderbilt's sister Eliza. The statue in front is of August Belmont, head of the New York branch of Rothschild's Bank; he is often credited with leading New York's high society to summer in Newport.

On the southwest corner of Bellevue is Rockry Hall, built in the Gothic Revival style for Albert Sumner in 1848, just two years before the town's great real estate developer, Alfred Smith, began building the fifty-foot-wide Bellevue Avenue, which he extended southward from here to the Atlantic ocean between 1851 and '53.

Going east on Narragansett Avenue, the pink-walled French-style chateau on the right was built in 1927 by architect Charles Adams Platt for the New York stockbroker William Fahnstock just two years before the Wall Street crash. Called Bois Dore, the mansion was recently owned by the late Catherine Skelly, heiress to an oil fortune.

The mansion at the end of the street on the left, called the Orchard, was built in 1871 as a copy of a French chateau for George Fearing—once the

Rockry Hall.

mayor of Newport. More recently, the Orchard was owned by the late Mrs. Harvey Firestone, the Firestone Rubber Company heiress, who used to keep this mansion as a buffer for privacy at her own mansion, Ocean Lawn (just behind it). Ocean Lawn was subsequently on the market for $5 million, and its contents were auctioned by Christie's of New York.

Ocean Lawn was built in 1889 by the Boston architect firm of Peabody and Stearns for Mr. William Gammell of Providence, heiress to the textile fortune of Goddard, Ives and Brown.

Turning right onto Ochre Point Avenue, on the left behind all the trees is Ochre Point Mansion, the largest of five Shingle-style houses being built between 1881 and '83 by McKim, Mead and White after completing the Newport Casino. It was built for Robert Goelet, who with his brother Ogden owned New York City real estate between Union Square at Fourteenth Street north to Forty-seventh Street with an estimated 1870 book value of $100 million.

Next on the left is Ochre Court, built for his brother Ogden Goelet nine years later by architect Richard Morris Hunt in the French Gothic Revival

Ochre Court.

style for a reported $4.5 million. Hunt, the first American architect to have graduated from the École des Beaux Arts in Paris, was also building three other large mansions here at the same time.

Ochre Court's three-story Great Hall has a ceiling painting showing the gods of Olympus holding a banquet, and the ceiling is supported by twelve Michelangelo-style figures holding it on their shoulders.

Today, this mansion is the Administration Building for Salve Regina, formerly a Roman Catholic girls' college that now admits men and owns a number of estates here. With more than 2,200 students, its tuition is over $20,000 per semester.

Vinland, the brownstone mansion on the left, was built by those prolific Boston architects Peabody and Sterns in 1883–84 for Catherine Lorillard Wolfe, a wealthy maiden who is said to have gotten so many marriage proposals that she had her calling card printed with the inscription "Not interested in matrimony!" as a warning to those hotheaded suitors.

Later, Vinland, which in the Norse language means "New World," was owned by Hamilton McKown Twombley, married to Florence Vanderbilt, Commodore Cornelius Vanderbilt's granddaughter.

Now it is owned by Salve Regina University, which was actually founded in Providence in 1934 by the Sisters of Mercy but moved to Newport in 1947, when the Goelet estate gave it Ochre Court. At the outset, I'm told it had fifty eight students sleeping on the third floor, while the faculty of eight nuns slept in the basement.

On the right is Wakehurst, built from 1882 to 1888 by local architect Dudley Newton for the railroad heir James L. Van Alen as a near copy of Wakehurst Place, built in 1590 in what is now part of Kew Gardens in London.

Van Alen is said to have loved everything English, not only filling the mansion with English furniture, but also filling his conversation with Shakespearean words—by him, a lovely lady would be called "a most delectable wench, forsooth!" His ambition to become U.S. minister to Italy was cut down after Joseph Pulitzer's *New York World* wrote a scathing editorial about Van Alen's "life among the idle rich."

And next on the grounds to the left is the university's new postmodern-style $7 million McKillop Library, with the latest computer research facilities. The university uses the mansion itself as a student center.

The spectacular Italian Renaissance palazzo-style mansion on the left, The Breakers, is the largest in Newport, covering just over half an acre on the first floor. With a full attic and basement, two levels of bedrooms

Wakehurst.

The Breakers.

and first-floor reception rooms, there are a total of seventy rooms—thirty-three for staff—roughly 138,00 square feet. The Great Hall and dining room each could accommodate a two-story house at nearly fifty feet in all three dimensions.

The Breakers was built for Cornelius Vanderbilt II, the oldest of four sons of William Henry Vanderbilt, who inherited $90 million of his father Commodore Cornelius Vanderbilt's $100 million railroad empire. But William Henry greatly expanded those railroads, leaving $200 million—$67 million to Cornelius II, $65 million to William K. Vanderbilt and $10 million each to the two younger sons and four daughters.

But it was Cornelius II's grandfather—the Commodore—who founded the family fortune with a $100 ferryboat on Staten Island, building a fleet of steamships over fifty years. Then, in 1862, he saw the future in railroads. He bought the Harlem River line and then the Hudson River line, extended service to Albany and Buffalo and, in 1875, established the White Mail train—New York to Chicago in only thirty-six hours!

Commodore Vanderbilt had thirteen children—eleven survived—but he left almost all his fortune to only one of his two surviving sons. He was thrifty and wouldn't see control of the railroads split up. When a gentleman asked why the commodore didn't buy a cigar case rather than stuffing cigars in his coat pockets, he said that with a cigar case people could see how many cigars he had. Without one, he would not have to "pass them around."

The Breakers was built in twenty-seven months by architect Richard Morris Hunt using some two thousand workers and twenty separate contractors. At the same time, Hunt was building the 255-room Biltmore in Ashville, North Carolina, for Cornelius II's youngest brother, George Washington Vanderbilt, and Mrs. Astor's new Fifth Avenue mansion, and he had already designed the Fifth Avenue main entrance of the Metropolitan Museum—and it killed him. He died on August 31, 1895, only three weeks before the first party was given at the Breakers.

Hunt had completed the reputed $11 million Marble House in August 1892 for Cornelius II's brother William, but two months later, when the original Breakers burned to the ground, Cornelius II's wife, Alice, suggested he hire the same architect to build them an even bigger house—and he did.

Appearing on the left as one turns right at the end of Ochre Point Avenue is Fairholme, the half Tudor-style mansion built in 1870 by architects Frank Furness and Allen Evans for the Philadelphian Fairman Rogers.

Rogers is credited with writing the authoritative rule book on the sport of coaching, which became most popular with gentlemen. In fact, for these Gilded Age socialites, the Sunday afternoon ritual was for the entire family to dress up in their finery, climb aboard their coaches drawn by four to six horses and parade up and down Bellevue Avenue.

Their coachmen were dressed in full livery and blew their trumpets as they distributed calling cards at neighbors' mansions. Of course, nobody was at home because they were all out doing the same thing.

Fairholme was later owned by the Philadelphia banker John R. Drexel I and later by Mr. and Mrs. Robert Young. The Youngs numbered among their guests the late Duke and Duchess of Windsor, and John F. Kennedy used to frequent their saltwater swimming pool.

In 1954, Young, with two partners, succeeded in wresting control of the New York Central Railroad from the Vanderbilt family. Perhaps by buying the house just across the street from The Breakers they were making a social statement?

Midcliff.

The next two Queen Anne–style mansions on the left, Midcliff and Honeysuckle Lodge, were both built in 1886 by the Boston architect firm of Peabody and Sterns for Joseph M. Fiske.

In the 1950s, Midcliff was owned by Perle Mesta, the Washington "hostess with the mostest," about whom the Broadway musical *Call Me Madame* was written. You may remember that she was a great fundraiser for Harry Truman, who appreciated her support and named her madame ambassador to Luxembourg. Honeysuckle Lodge was later owned by the great amateur of the 1930s, T. Suffern Tailer.

The next sixteenth-century French Norman Gothic–style limestone mansion on the left, which boasts some forty bedrooms and twenty bathrooms among its fifty-four rooms, was completed in 1925 for $2 million not long before the 1929 Wall Street crash by architect Howard Greenly for Edson Bradley.

Bradley claimed his fortune came from mining, but it was probably mostly from distilling whiskey and other alcoholic liquors. The mansion also has a chapel seating nearly one hundred for Bradley's son-in-law, Bishop Shipman of New York, who served as chaplain at West Point and wrote the West Point hymn "The Core."

Later, the estate was brought by Martin Carey, brother of former New York governor Hugh Carey, who dreamed of finding oil off George's Bank and reportedly bought this for his oil company headquarters. Not finding oil, he leased those forty bedrooms to Salve Regina for use as a dormitory until recent years.

The house also served as the stage setting for the 1960 TV thriller *Dark Shadows*.

## Bellevue Avenue—South

The Elizabethan-style brownstone manor house on the left as one turns south on Bellevue Avenue from Ruggles Avenue is called Fairlawn. The left side of house was built in 1852 by Seth Branford, a local contractor for Andrew Ritichie, but it was enlarged in 1869 by architect Richard Morris Hunt for Levi P. Morton.

Morton was planning a banquet for Ulysses S. Grant to celebrate Grant's election as president of the United States the previous November. Twenty years later, Morton was elected vice president of the United States with our twenty-third president, Benjamin Harrison (1889–93).

Fairlawn.

Near the turn of the century, Fairlawn was owned by Townsend Burden, whose family fortune came from iron. It was Mrs. Burden who was credited with introducing the court jester of later Gilded Age parties, Harry Lehr, to his first taste of high society in this house.

It was *the* Mrs. Astor who is said to have approved Harry as a spouse for the very wealthy Elizabeth Drexel, only for Elizabeth to be told by Harry on her wedding night that he had "just married her for her money." She kept up that marriage fiction for twenty-nine years, until Harry finally died of cancer. Her mother had a heart condition and was a strict Catholic. Elizabeth was afraid a divorce would kill her.

The new stone mansion on the left stands on the site of Bythesea, a mansion built in 1860 for August Belmont, who came to New York in 1873 at the age of twenty-three and soon opened a branch of the Rothschild's Bank in that city. He married the daughter of Admiral Matthew Perry, who in 1854 was credited with negotiating the first treaty with Japan—the first step in opening that country to the West.

He introduced ten-course dinners and servants dressed in full livery like those in European palaces to his Newport mansion, and some credit him with making this town the summer capital for the high-fashion wealthy. Perhaps that's why the Preservation Society has placed his bronze statue in front of its headquarters building on Bellevue Avenue at Narragansett Avenue.

Next on the left is the beautifully proportioned Rosecliff, modeled after Louis XIV's Grand Trianon Versailles garden palace by architect Stanford White. This was the stage for such movies as *The Great Gatsby* with Robert Redford and Mia Farrow; *The Betsy* with Robert Duvall, Sir Lawrence Olivier and Katherine Ross; and *True Lies* with Arnold Schwarzenegger and Mary Lee Curtis.

Rosecliff was built between 1898 and 1902 for $2.5 million for the beautiful Mrs. Herman Oelrich and Virginia Fair, daughters of James Fair, who along with three partners discovered some $200 million worth of silver, called the Comstock Lode, in Virginia City, Nevada. Mr. Oelrich died of a heart attack on one of his ships only four years after the house was completed.

Rosecliff.

In a society coup engineered by her sister, Theresa Fair Oelrich, Virginia married William K. Vanderbilt's oldest son, Willie Jr., down at Marble House when Rosecliff was only a year under construction. Assisting in that society coup was Willie's mother, Alva Erskin Smith Vanderbilt.

Rosecliff was later owned by J. Edgar Monroe, who made a fortune in Louisiana sugar plantations and oil wells and in 1972 gave this mansion with a generous endowment to the Preservation Society. Generous, indeed!

And looking a bit like the White House, the Georgian-style mansion on the right, called Sherwood, was given the present look and name in a 1906 renovation for Mr. and Mrs. Pembroke Jones of New Orleans by Colonel Francis Hoppin, who had earlier apprenticed under McKim, Mead and White in New York.

Sherwood was originally in the Tudor style with half timbering when it was built in 1872 for Loring Andrews and originally given the name Friedheim. It was bought in 1880 by Theodore Havermeyer of the Domino Sugar Company.

Continuing down Bellevue Avenue, on the left you can see Beechwood, built in 1852 by architects Calvert Vaux and Andrew Jackson Downing for the New York dry goods merchant Daniel Parish.

But Beechwood was bought in 1881 for $190,000 by Mrs. William Backhouse Astor Jr., who had been promoted by Ward McAllister, of Savannah, Georgia, to limit New York and Newport high society to four hundred who would "feel at ease in a ballroom" without making others

Beechwood Mansion.

"uneasy in the same room." She named twenty-five "patriarchs from old New York families" to make that selection and then "scrutinize them for worthiness" in the next round of invitations.

Mrs. Astor then hired architect Richard Hunt for a $2 million remodeling, including a ballroom holding four hundred—just like the one in her Fifth Avenue mansion.

In recent years, Beechwood has been open to the public, with a group of professional actors pretending to be servants of Mrs. William Backhouse Astor Jr. (née Caroline Webster Schermerhorn) greeting you like you were her guests coming to call during the Gilded Age.

Then, in January 2012, Larry Ellison, co-founder of Oracle Corporation, bought Beechwood for $10.5 million and has unveiled plans to restore the mansion and enhance the elaborate gardens, converting them into the Beechwood Art Museum. It would then host his collection of eighteenth- and nineteenth-century artworks. Plans for the restoration of Beechwood and its use as a public museum are under review by Newport government agencies.

According to *Forbes* magazine, Ellison is the third-richest person in America with a net worth of $33 billion, exceeded only by Bill Gates of Microsoft and Warren Buffett of Berkshire Hathaway. And Ellison also owns the yacht that won the 2010 America's Cup competition. Upon completing all of his proposed improvements, he might even out break the Breakers—to the joy of Mrs. Astor.

Next on the left is the $11 million Marble House modeled after the Petite Trianon at Versailles by architect Hunt for William K. Vanderbilt, who gave the new mansion to his wife, Alva, as a gift on her thirty-ninth birthday. Unfortunately, three years later, she divorced him after twenty years of marriage and three children on grounds of adultery, which he did not choose to contest. Actually, these were the only grounds on which a divorce could be granted in New York State at the time.

And only a year afterward, Alva married their best friend, Oliver Hazard Perry Belmont, and moved into Belcourt, which Oliver reportedly gave to her as a wedding present. Now she had two mansions in Newport, both of which had been built at the same time by the same architect, Richard Hunt. Alva allowed her oldest son, William K. Jr., to occupy Marble House with his new bride, Virginia Faie, from Rosecliff, while she lived in Belcourt until Oliver's death twelve years later, in 1908.

Alva then went to battle to win the right for women to vote, renting an office building in New York City for the women's suffrage movement and

Marble House.

buying it a headquarters buildings not only in Washington, D.C., but also in Paris and Rome.

She also served as president of the National Women's Party and led five thousand women down Fifth Avenue from Central Park to Washington Square on the Inauguration Day of Woodrow Wilson so he wouldn't get all the headlines.

Alva's wish that a female clergyman would conduct her funeral service, which was held in New York's St. Thomas Episcopal Church (she died at the age of eighty in 1933), was not carried out, but forty women, all representing women's rights organizations, were there to honor her. And they all sang the "Women's Rights Hymn," which she had written: "No waiting at the Gates of Paradise; No tribunal of petty men to rule!"

The next large Second Empire–style mansion on the left with that concave mansard roof is called Beaulieu, which translates to "Beautiful Place." It was built in 1859 by New York architect Calvert Vaux for the Peruvian ambassador, Frederick L. de Barreda.

John Jacob Astor III got the lion's share of the $40 million estate of his father, William Backhouse Astor Sr., on the latter's death in 1875 and soon

Beaulieu Mansion.

followed the society summer rush to Newport by buying Beaulieu. Not to be outdone, in 1881, Caroline, the wife of his younger brother (William B. Jr.), bought Beechwood and gave architect Hunt $2 million for that remodeling job with a ballroom for only four hundred.

Being married to the older and wealthier son (much of their wealth stemmed from tenements built by their father for New York's exploding population of immigrants), Charlotte had the right to the family title of *the* Mrs. Astor over her sister-in-law Caroline.

Upon Charlotte's death in 1887, J.J. Astor III gave Beaulieu to his son William Waldorf Astor, whose wife, Mary Dahlgren Paul, was entitled to inherit the title of the Mrs. Astor. But her niece by marriage, Carolyn, also claimed it. The postman never knew whether to deliver *the* Mrs. Astor's mail to Beaulieu or Beechwood. The problem was solved when William Waldorf and his wife moved to England in 1901 and joined the British nobility as Viscount Astor of Hever Castle. He had sold Beaulieu to Cornelius Vanderbilt III, known as Nealey. Nealey, who had been disinherited of the Breakers by his father, received only $1.5 million, because of his marriage to Grace Wilson. It was alleged that this was because Cornelius II thought

Grace's father—who made a fortune in banking and restoring southern railroads—was a Civil War profiteer.

The $37 million inheritance Cornelius III had expected did go to his younger brother Alfred, who in 1915 was among the 1,200 souls lost in the *Lusitania* sinking.

Next on the left and opposite Rovinskey Park is Clarendon Court, built in 1904 for Edward C. Knight, whose family owned the Pullman (railway) Palace Car Company. He named this French Beaux-Arts-style mansion Claradon Court after his first wife, Clara.

It was Claus von Bulow who changed the mansion's name to Clarendon Court after his wife, Sunny, bought it. It was here in this mansion, of course, that Claus was twice accused of trying to murder his wife by insulin injection, but Alan Dershowitz won his acquittal during the second trial. The front elevation of the house was also used as a set in the Grace Kelley movie *High Society*. The architect for Clarendon Court was Horace Trumbauer, who designed not only the Elms for Edward Berwin but also the next carriage house and mansion on the left—Miramar—for Mrs. George Weidner.

Miramar was designed for George, whose father, P.A.B. Widener, made the family fortune from streetcars operating in Philadelphia, New York and Chicago. After George and his son Harry were drowned in the sinking of the *Titanic* in 1912, Mrs. Widener asked Trumbauer to proceed with the

Clarendon Court.

Miramar.

building of Miramar, as well as the Widener Library at Harvard University, the latter in their memory.

The large mansion behind the wall on the right is Belcourt Castle, built in 1901 with fifty-five rooms and thirty-four horse stalls by Richard Hunt at the same time he was building Marble House, Ochre Court and Wrentham House (on Ocean Drive)—four mansions at once here in Newport.

This is the Louis XIII–style hunting lodge Alva Vanderbilt moved into when she divorced William K. and married her best friend, Oliver Hazard Perry Belmont. Oliver, the fun-loving third and least successful son of August Belmont, was earlier—against his parents' wishes—married to Sarah Swan Whiting of Swanhurst Mansion on Bellevue. In the earlier marriage, Oliver and Sarah had barely moved into their Paris hotel honeymoon suite when Sarah's mother and two unmarried sisters moved in with them. Oliver couldn't get them to move out and in a pique of anger ran off to Spain with another woman.

Oliver's mother, Carolyn, the daughter of Commodore Matthew Perry, couldn't put that marriage back together again.

In building Belcourt, Oliver had Trumbauer put stables for thirty-four of his beloved horses right on the first floor, but Alva eventually persuaded him to build the stables next door. And Alva moved the location of the mansion's grand staircase so many times that local horse-drawn tour bus guides used to tell tourists about it through their megaphones when they stopped outside.

Belcourt Castle.

Alva thought this was so amusing that she once asked the guests at her luncheon party to "be still and listen." Unfortunately, the guide that day had changed his spiel. "This," he said, "is the home of Alva Smith Vanderbilt Belmont. She used to dwell in marble halls with Mr. Vanderbilt. But after dragging her husband through the divorce courts, she now lives over the stables with Mr. Belmont." Her face must have turned several shades of red, but what could she say then?

As Bellevue Avenue turns to the right, the great English Tudor–style mansion on that outside corner is called Rough Point, built by those busy Boston architects Peabody and Stern for Frederick William Vanderbilt who, like his younger brother George Washington Vanderbilt, inherited only $10 million when their father William Henry died. It was Cornelius II and William K. who inherited more than $60 million each.

But Fred actually turned his $10 million into more than $70 million in banking, and George got Richard Hunt to build the largest of their mansions—the Biltmore in Asheville, North Carolina, with 255 rooms, as well as a winery and the beginnings of a forestry service.

In 1923, two years before his death, Rough Point was bought by James Buchanan Duke, who with his brother had founded the American Tobacco

Rough Point.

Company. His young daughter eventually came into the fortune and, on her death in 1993, left an estate of some $1.2 billion.

That estate had to fight claims of her adopted daughter, whom she renounced before her death, and her butler, whom she had named trustee of her estate. After being removed as trustee, the butler appealed the decision in court, and won the appeal, but then died after spending only a few million dollars. (She was also a friend of Imelda Marcos, the late Philippine dictator who had a large collection of shoes.)

In 1968, Doris Duke founded the Newport Restoration Foundation, one of three major historical organizations here, and over the succeeding years saved more than eighty colonial period homes in Newport. The NRF leases them out privately with historical restrictions.

In 2000, the NRF opened Rough Point for tours on which you may also view Duke's grand collection of paintings and tapestries, including some by Thomas Gainsborough and Joshua Reynolds.

At the end of Bellevue, the white-columned Colonial Revival–style mansion on the right is called Beachmound. It was built in 1897 by architect Henry I. Cobb for Benjamin Thaw, a relative of Harry Thaw.

Beachmound.

Harry was that wealthy psychotic playboy who murdered one of America's greatest early twentieth-century architects, Stanford White, during a musical performance on June 25, 1906, in front of a crowd of two hundred people on the roof garden of the original New York Madison Square Garden building, which White had designed.

Thaw had married White's former girlfriend, Evelyn Nesbit. To make Harry jealous, Evelyn told him White had boasted that he would win back her affections. Harry cut short that effort by walking up to White's table and shooting him three times in the head. Turning to Evelyn, Harry said, "The man will never bother you again."

Harry was found innocent on grounds of insanity, but after serving eight years in an asylum, he was released as "sane."

## Beginning of Ocean Drive

Turning left onto Ocean Drive, one can see Bailey's Beach, possibly amongst the most exclusive beaches in the world. They say you can't join. You have to inherit a cabana, as well as pay for it. Ted Kennedy is reported to have once sailed his sunfish onto the beach property and been thrown out.

The beach for rejects and ordinary mortals is the one just before Bailey's to the east.

The mansion on top of the hill at the right is naturally called High Tide. It was built in 1900 for William Starr Miller by local architect Whitney Warren, who also designed the present Grand Central Station in New York City and the Biltmore Hotel in Providence, Rhode Island.

High Tide was later owned by Joseph W. Frazier, who, with his partner Henry Kaiser, invented the World War II Jeep and the Kaiser Frazer automobile. (Anyone remember them now?)

Crossways, the mansion on the next hill at the right, with that great Colonial Revival portico supported by white columns, was built in 1898 by local architect Dudley Newton.

It was built for Mrs. Stuyvesant Fish, known by her friends as Mamie. When *the* Mrs. Astor retired as queen of New York and Newport High

Bailey's Beach Club.

High Tide.

Crossways Mansion.

Society, her throne was grabbed by Mamie, Tessie Oelrich and Alva Vanderbilt Belmont.

These ladies even had a different sense of humor. One day, Alva accused Mamie of telling Tessie that she, being a bit plump, "looked like a frog." "No, no," Mamie said. "Never told her you looked like a frog. I told her you looked like a toad!"

The most far out and outrageous of the three—who came to be known as society's "Triumvirate Rulers"—was Mamie. One day, she invited one hundred guests to a dinner for their...dogs! And she got a kick out of going up to one of her guests and saying, "I forgot I invited you. Do make yourself at home as there is no one who wishes you were there more than I do." With friends like that, who worries about enemies?

The next two beach clubs, Gooseberry and Hazard, are private or semi-private.

Gooseberry Landing, the island off to the left, used to be called Millionaires' Island because when the Newport Fishing Club held parties there, more wealth was said to be on the island at one time than was in the entire rest of the country. No doubt an overstatement, but they represented a lot of money.

There were only fifteen members paying $1,500 a year for seafood dinners. The 1938 hurricane took out the original clubhouse. Later, the island was bought by Beverley Bogart, of Anglesea Mansion, who liked to entertain the likes of Liz Taylor, Frank Sinatra and John F. Kennedy.

The mansion Eagles Nest was built in 1924 by the architectural firm of Aldrich and Sleeper for F. Frazier Jelke, of the Oleo margarine fortune.

The next mansion you see through the arched gatehouse on the left, called Normandy, was built in 1914 by architect William Adams Delano for Mrs. Lucy Wortham James.

And the next mansion on the left with all those chimneys is called Seafare; it was built in 1937 by architect William MacKenzie for Verner Z. Reed Jr., heir to a Colorado silver mine fortune. His wife at one time owned the unlucky Hope Diamond. It brought several of its owners bad luck.

Seafare survived the 1938 hurricane when the house was just a year old, but five servants, who apparently tried to flee the mansion during that horrendous storm, were all drowned. Afterward, the Reed family never came back to the property.

Behind the long-needled mango pine trees on the left is Wildacre, built in 1901 by the California architect Irving Gill for Albert Olmsted, whose father, Frederick Law Olmsted, designed, among others, New York's Central

Eaglesnest.

Normandy.

Seafare.

Wildacre.

Park, the Boston Public Gardens, Philadelphia's Fairmont Park, the 1892 Columbia Exposition grounds, parts of Newport's Ocean Drive and the gardens around Hammersmith Farm, where John F. Kennedy held his wedding reception with Jackie.

Fitted into the landscape is the Wrentham House, built in 1891 for J.R. Busk by Richard Hunt while he was building Ochre Court, Marble House and Belcourt. He was one busy architect, but of course, he had a large office staff in New York to help him out.

Turning down Harrison Avenue to the right, farther down on the right is the Newport Country Club, the site of many great parties.

It was built in 1894 by Whitney Warren, his first project after returning the previous year from studying at the Paris École des Beaux Arts. His design was chosen over that of seventy other architects.

The club hosted the first U.S. Open Golf competition and was founded by Theodore Havermeyer, who first cornered the New York sugar market with Domino Sugar. The building caught the attention of another club leader: William K. Vanderbilt, who in 1913 hired Warren to build the present New York Grand Central Station.

The Newport Country Club.

Continuing along Ocean Drive, the dirt road on the left goes out on the point, called Price's Neck, which has long been a favorite spot for fishermen. It was the site of the U.S. Coast Guard Newport station until it was destroyed by the 1938 hurricane.

And in the ocean water to the left is where America's Cup yacht races were run by the New York Yacht Club here in Newport from 1930 until 1983. Starting from here, the races took place on a course between a series of buoys from five to twelve miles out. The first to take four out of a possible seven races got to keep the cup until the next series—held usually every three or four years.

Originally named the Guinea or Common Cup during a race off the coast of Britain's Isle of Wight—a fifty-eight-mile race—the prize was brought home by the New York Yacht Club, and it kept it for all of 132 years, until Dennis Conner lost it to Australia's James Bond in 1883. That's when the New York Yacht Club stopped writing the rules of the competition. That seems to have made a difference. The New York club hasn't been able to win the cup back since then!

Off to the left as one rounds the curve to the right is Brenton Point State Park, named after William Brenton, one of some thirty founders of Newport in 1639 and now part of the eighty-nine-acre park that bears his name.

In the park at the right, one can see the new monument to Portuguese explorers of New England. It commemorates the many local fishermen who have drowned at sea over more than three and a half centuries.

Beyond the little cluster of cabins down the road to the left is the Inn on Castle Hill, today a classy inn and restaurant. It was built in 1874 for Alexander Agassiz, a Harvard professor and founder of Harvard's Museum of Comparative Zoology. He is frequently called the first marine zoologist in America.

The U.S. Coast Guard Station on the left was built in 1940 to replace the one destroyed in the 1938 hurricane.

Next on the left is Oceancliff, now expanded with those new buildings to operate as a timeshare apartment house and restaurant. The original name was Shamrock Cliff when it was built in 1896 by the Boston architects Peabody and Sterns for Guam Hutton, an American diplomat who married a railroad heiress.

The next mansion on the left, called Broadlawns, was built in 1882 for Josiah Low. It is said to have become famous during Prohibition, when state police continuously raided it on suspicion that the new owners were

The Inn on Castle Hill.

Oceancliff.

Broadlawns.

conducting an illegal gambling operation. The operators claimed that they were only operating a school for men to learn how to operate a gambling casino, which was not illegal.

Next on the left is Hammersmith Farm, used by President Kennedy as a summer White House but owned by Jackie Bouvier's stepfather, Hugh Auchincloss. The rambling house has a magnificent view of the Newport Harbor entrance, as well as twenty-eight rooms, seventeen bathrooms and thirty-five fireplaces.

Hammersmith was built in 1888 by architect R.H. Robertson for John W. Auchincloss, while Olmsted Brothers constructed its elaborate gardens. This was the site of John F. Kennedy's wedding reception for 1,300 guests on September 12, 1953. While open for public tours for more than a dozen years, it is now a private residence.

Hammersmith Farm.

## HARRISON AVENUE AND HARBOR FRONT

On the left is Fort Adams, named after our second president and first built in 1799. It was twice enlarged by the Scottish stonemason Alexander Macgregor, who also built the Artillery Company Museum, the Perry Mill and St. Mary's Roman Catholic Church, where John F. Kennedy married Jackie.

The fort is the oldest bastion fort on the East Coast. It was built to defend Narragansett Bay from enemy ships, as well as from attack by land. It could quarter up to 2,400 troops and bristled with 468 cannons—which were rendered obsolete when cannons with rifling in the barrels were developed during the Civil War. These could have pulverized the walls of the fort if it were attacked.

Part of the fort is now open for public tours. It features the Newport Yachting Museum and sailing lessons and serves as a public amphitheater for the Newport Jazz and Folk Festivals each summer.

On the grounds, you will find the house built by architect George Champlin Mason in 1873 for the fort commander. Now leased for private receptions, it once served as President Dwight D. Eisenhower's summer house.

On top of the next cliff overlooking the bay is Beacon Rock. Recently, it was the home of the famous sculptor Felix de Weldon, best known for the Iwo Jima Monument showing three U.S. marines struggling to raise the American flag during that famous World War II battle with the Japanese.

The mansion itself was built in 1889 by McKim, Mead and White for former New York State governor and senator Edwin D. Morgan Jr.

If you look behind you on the right, you can see the reproduction of a Swiss village built for Arthur Curtis James, a railroad magnate, as a "surprise" for his wife to celebrate their sixth honeymoon.

Mrs. James had so greatly enjoyed their fifth honeymoon trip to Switzerland that James was determined to build a Swiss-style village, equipped with sheep and peasants right on his Newport estate. The mansion has since been torn down.

The forty-five-acre village was purchased in 1998 and now serves as the Swiss Village Farm Foundation, (SVF), established by Campbell Soup heiress

Fort Adams State Park.

Beacon Rock.

Dorrance Hill Hamilton. SVF has renovated the farm buildings, which now serve as facilities for preserving some 4,500 samples of germ plasma from sheep, goats and cattle, and the farm is now dedicated to the preservation of genetically diverse livestock in conjunction with Tufts University.

On the right is Edgehill, in more recent times a drug and alcohol rehabilitation clinic, which was modeled after the Betty Ford Clinic. More recently, it was used as a horse-breeding farm. It was built in 1887 by McKim, Mead and White for George Gordon King of Newport's King family.

After rounding the corner to the left, you will see Beachbound, built by those prolific architects Peabody and Sterns for William F. Burden, and after turning to the right, you will see on the left Bonnicrest Mansion, with its many chimneys.

Bonnicrest was built in 1918 by architect John Russell Pope, who also designed the Jefferson Memorial and the National Gallery of Art in Washington, D.C. It was built for Stewart Duncan of Lee and Perrins Worcestershire sauce fame. You have all used it! An enterprising Newport

Beachbound.

Bonnicrest Mansion.

roof slater named Louis Chartier made so much money repairing slate roofs of Newport's many mansions after the 1938 hurricane that he was able to buy this one, as well as several others, and convert them into rental apartments.

Bonnicrest has now been turned into condominiums, and two additional buildings have been constructed on the site where some of Frederick Law Olmsted's landscape gardens were located. For this monstrous destruction, Bonnicrest was stricken from the National Register of Historic Places.

Turning left onto Wellington Avenue, you will see Harbor Court, the John Nicholas Brown estate built in 1904 by the architects Cram, Ferguson and Gooodhue, who also built New York's Cathedral of St. John the Divine and St. Bartholomew's Church.

The Brown family, in colonial times, was heavily engaged in slave trading, but the family also endowed Brown University, in Providence, Rhode Island, and gave the university its name.

Harbor Court recently became the Newport home of the New York Yacht Club, and the flagpole in front of the building is actually the mast from the yacht *America*, which won the America's Cup from the British entry *Aurora* in

Harbor Court Mansion.

The Ida Lewis Yacht Club.

1851 by about eight minutes. (See the biography of James Gordon Bennett, who won it.)

Rounding the corner, you can see the Ida Lewis Yacht Club out on that little island. It was named after the first female lighthouse keeper in America. Her father had been the keeper of the lighthouse, which was then known as the Old Lime Rock Lighthouse. In his absence in 1854, at the age of twelve and during a storm, Ida used her boat to rescue four men whose boat had sunk in the harbor.

President Ulysses S. Grant traveled to Newport to present her with the Congressional Medal of Honor for her heroism. Ida remained the lighthouse keeper here until her death in 1911 at age sixty-nine.

Again overlooking the harbor on the left is King's Park, where you can see a bronze statue of the French General de Rochambeau, who landed right here with six thousand French soldiers from 434 ships in 1780. His statue was dedicated in 1911.

Among Newport's older buildings are part of the John Mawdsley House (1680), part of the Quaker Meetinghouse (originally with a tower on top;

A statue of the French General de Rochambeau.

1699), part of the Whitehouse Tavern on Farewell Street (1673), Trinity Church (1725), the Second Congregational Church on Clark Street (1735), St. Paul's Methodist Church on Marlboro Street (1806), the Walton-Lyman-Hazard House on Broadway (1775) and perhaps the Old Stone Mill on Touro Park (by the twelfth-century Vikings).

## Coachman's Favorite Old Inns and Restaurants

### *Hotels with Spas and Pools*

Newport Marriott, adjacent to the Visitors' Center
Hyatt Regency, just to the west on Goat Island
Newport Harbor Hotel and Marina, just to the south
Viking Hotel, 1 Bellevue Avenue

### *Bed-and-Breakfasts*

Cliffside Inn, 2 Seaview Terrace, 847-1811
Inn on Castle Hill, 590 Ocean Avenue, 549-3800
Sanford Covell House, 72 Washington Street, 847-0206
Francis Malbone House, 392 Thames Street, 846-0392
Bellevue House, 14 Catherine Street, 847-1828
Chandler at Cliffwalk, 117 Memorial Boulevard, 847-1300
LaFarge Perry House, 24 Kay Street, 847-2223
Black Duck Inn, 29 Pelham Street, 847-4400
Jailhouse Inn, 13 Marlborough Street, 847-4638
Architect's Inn Bliss, 31 Old Beach Road, 847-7081

### *Restaurants*

White Horse Tavern, Marlborough Street, 849-3600
Black Pearl, Bannister's Wharf, 846-5264
Clark Cooke House, Bannister's Wharf, 849-2900
Inn on Castle Hill. 590 Ocean Avenue, 849-3800
Perro Salado, 19 Charles Street, 619-4777

Bouchard's, 505 Thames Street, 846-0123
Salvation Cafe, 140 Broadway, 847-2620
Fifth Element, 111Broadway, 619-2552
Canfield House, 5 Memorial Boulevard, 847-0416
La Forge Casino, 186 Bellevue Avenue, 847-0418

## *Parks*

Cliff Walk, 3.5 miles; park on Narragansett Avenue to avoid fines
Fort Adams State Park, Harrison Avenue
Brenton State Park, Ocean Avenue
Norman Bird Sanctuary, Memorial Boulevard to Paradise Avenue
Green Animals Topiary Gardens, North on Route 114, 9 miles to Corey Lane

# BIBLIOGRAPHY


Baker, Paul. *Richard Morris Hunt*. Cambridge, MA: MIT Press, 1980.

———. *Stanny: The Gilded Life of Stanford White*. New York: Free Press, a Division of McMillan, Inc., 1989.

Balsan, Consuelo Vanderbilt. *The Glitter and the Gold*. New York: Harper & Bros., n.d.

Black, David. *The King of Fifth Avenue: The Fortunes of August Belmont*. New York: Dial Press, 1981.

Crockett, Albert Stevens. *When James Gordon Bennett Was Caliph of Baghdad*. New York: Funk & Wagnalls Co., 1926.

Downing, Antoinette, and Vincent Scully Jr. *The Architectural Heritage of Newport, RI, 1640–1915*. 2nd ed. New York, 1967.

Elliott, Maude Howe. *This Was My Newport*. Cambridge, MA: Mythology Co., 1944.

*Encyclopedia Britannica*. Chicago: William Brenton, 1966.

Gilmartin, Gregory F. *Shaping the City: New York & Municipal Art Society*. New York: Clarkso Potter, Publishers, 1995.

Grafton, John. *New York in the 19th Century*. New York: Dover Publications, Inc., 1980.

Jefferys, C.P.B. *Newport: A Short History*. Portsmouth, RI: Hamilton Printing Co., 1992.

Lowe, David Garrard. *Stanford White's New York*. New York: Doubleday, 1992.

Lowenthal, Larry. "The Cliff Walk at Newport." *Newport History* 61, part 4, no. 212 (1988).

McAlester, Virginia, and Lee McAlester. *A Field Guide to American Houses*. New York: Alfred A. Knopf, 1984.

O'Connor, Richard. *The Scandalous Mr. Bennett.* Garden City, NY: Double Day, 1962.

Patterson, Jerry. *The Vanderbilts*. New York: Harry N. Abrams, Inc., 1989.

Schumacher, Alan T. "The Newport Casino, Its History." *Newport History* 61, part 2, no. 206 (1987).

Seitz, Don Carlos. *The James Gordon Bennetts, Father and Son: Proprietors of the* New York Herald. Indianapolis: Bobbs-Merrill Co., 1928.

Silver, Nathan. *Lost City of New York*. New York: Wings Books, 1967.

Sinclair, David. *Dynasty: The Astors and Their Times*. New York: Beaufort Books, 1984.

Tschirch, John. Preservation Society of Newport County Study Guides for The Breakers, Marble House, Rosecliff, Chateau Sur Mer, and The Elms. Newport, 1997.

Vanderbilt, Cornelius, Jr. *Queen of the Golden Age*. London: George Mann of Maidstone, 1956.

*Webster's Biographical Dictionary*. Springfield, MA: G&C Mirriam Co., 1943.

Winslow, John G. "Winslow Oral History Project." *Newport History* 68, part l, no. 234 (1997). Interviews with Daniel Snydacker Jr., executive director, Newport Historical Society.

Wurman, Richard Saul. *The Newport Guide*. Newport, RI: Initial Press Syndicate, n.d.

# ABOUT THE AUTHOR

Ed Morris is a veteran reporter for two Connecticut newspapers and was a correspondent for the United Press International's Berlin Bureau just before the construction of the Berlin Wall by Communist East Germany. A graduate of Wesleyan University in Middletown, Connecticut, he has also served as a tour guide for several Newport historical organizations for many years.

As a step-on bus guide for cruise ship visitors to Newport, he developed this coachman's script twelve years ago. After showing it to Pieter Roos, then education director of the Newport Historical Society, he was hired to research Newport's Cliff Walk and give tours to Newport tourists for six years. That tour, published as *A Guide to Newport's Cliff Walk*, has sold over seven thousand copies.

This companion volume is enlivened with more stories about those rogues and heroes of Newport's Gilded Age. Morris has made extensive use of the Newport Historical Society's research facilities, printed reports and many other sources, but the responsibility for the material contained herein is his own.